A JOB FOR ALL SEASONS

My Small Country Living

For Duff

A JOB FOR
ALL SEASONS

My Small Country Living

Phyllida Barstow

Illustrated by Lucy Milne

MERLIN UNWIN BOOKS

First published by Merlin Unwin Books, 2013

Merlin Unwin Books Ltd
Palm
Ludl
www

The right of P   thor
of this work I   with
the Copyrigh

A CIP recor(itish
Library.

Printed and bound by TJ International Ltd, Padstow, England

ISBN 978-1-906122-55-3

CONTENTS

CHAPTER ONE

On the Strength

LAYERS FOR SALE. 2/6d EACH proclaimed a tatty cardboard notice pinned to a gatepost I passed daily on the school run. Each? Even in the early 1960s this seemed absurdly cheap for a whole live chicken, when a 3lb roaster still cost several pounds. Since moving from London to Oxfordshire the previous year, we had once or twice mentioned keeping hens, but so far done nothing about it.

Half-a-crown each? How could one go wrong? On impulse I turned in the direction of the pointing arrow and drove down a bumpy track between unkempt hedges into a muddy yard flanked by three long, grey, asbestos sheds.

For such a knockdown price, I wasn't expecting show specimens, but even so I was shocked when I saw what the burly, green-overalled baldie in the little wooden office was selling.

'How many d'you want?' he asked, lumbering from his chair.

'Well... six, I should think.' Having made no preparations for housing them, I didn't want to overdo the numbers.

'Make it eight – that'll be a quid,' he said jovially. 'They're good birds, mind. Eighteen months old. Plenty of lay in 'em still.'

'Oh, OK. Thanks.'

I followed him across the yard. When he opened the heavy steel door of the first shed, a blast of thick, hot, ammoniac air assailed my nose, a combination of dust, feathers and chicken-droppings made my eyes stream, and we stepped into a scene to haunt any animal lover's nightmares. Under the roof of corrugated perspex, a double wall of wire cages as high as you could reach, separated by a narrow aisle, stretched away to the end of the shed like apartment blocks in New York, making you feel as if walking in a canyon. In each cage, whose sloping floor was no bigger than a sheet of typing paper, were crammed five clucking, cackling, jostling, pellet-pecking chickens, their constantly-moving heads pale brown, their staring eyes round and mad, and their bodies almost completely naked.

Working methodically along the line of grille-like shelves that formed an extension to the cage-floor, two lank-haired youths were collecting the eggs that had rolled out through a narrow gap at the bottom and come to rest against a small ledge just out of the birds' reach. Now and again they would open a door, reach in and remove a sick or dead hen, throwing it into a barrow full of grey-white guano, then quickly relatching the cage door.

The din was incessant, the heat and smell overpowering, and the continually bobbing heads made me feel sick and dizzy, liable to suffocate or vomit. I wished I had never turned off the road. How could people work in a place like this? How could anyone treat living creatures in such a way?

'This here's the batch to go,' said my guide, stopping at the end of the aisle. 'There's a new lot coming in Wednesday, so we'll be wanting to clear this section.'

I felt too zombified to ask what would happen to the birds he didn't sell. It seemed unlikely that one small notice would attract buyers for several hundred birds before Wednesday.

'Go on,' he urged. 'Plenty of choice. Pick what you want.'

'I'll leave it to you,' I gulped, struggling with nausea.

'Right, then. Ten, wasn't it?'

'Eight.' I would have liked to take the lot and release them into some form of chicken paradise, but just retained enough grip on reality to see that even eight was more than we needed, and some urgent carpentry was going to occupy the next few days if the poor creatures were to be decently housed.

He nodded and ran an expert eye over the cages' occupants, pulling out a bird here and there, holding them by the legs in one hand until he had enough. It reminded me horribly of a guard at a Nazi concentration camp deciding which prisoners were fit to work and which should go to the gas chambers.

'Right,' he said after a couple of minutes. 'These'll do you. Got a box in the car? Don't worry. I'll find something,' and preceded me out to the blessed fresh air.

When I got home an hour later and opened the flimsy cardboard carton, the birds looked more of a liability than a bargain. Huddled miserably on top of one another, naked and scrawny, they were obviously feeling the change in temperature and, although it was mid July, I abandoned any plans to put them outside in a shed for the night. Instead we rigged up temporary quarters in an old playpen beside the boiler, but even when I placed them on its floor they continued to crouch while pecking frantically at the pellets in a dish in front of them, having apparently lost the use of their legs.

They had left inside the carton two brown eggs.

Seventy weeks of close confinement had eradicated all normal chicken behaviour apart from the functions of eating and laying, recycling food into eggs as automatically as machines, and voiding the residue. Their feet were lily-white, with soft nails, quite unlike the tough, scaly, yellowish legs and sharp claws of free-rangers, and their beaks had been clipped short to discourage them from pecking out their mates' feathers – not that that particular mutilation seemed to have had much effect, seeing their semi-naked condition. They had never heard the clucking of their mother or copied her in scratching the soil. They had never been given the opportunity to preen their feathers or scuffle luxuriously in a dustbath. They had never even breathed properly-fresh air. Suspended above the ground in perpetual light, barely able to move, they knew nothing of the changing seasons or the difference between night and day, and whenever they laid an egg, it had rolled out of their reach before they could brood it for even a moment.

For the past seventy weeks, in effect, they had existed rather than lived. Whether they still had the capacity to revert to normality seemed, at that point, far from certain.

By next morning two had keeled over and lay stiffly, necks extended – killed, I imagine, by the sudden change in conditions – but the others had begun to shuffle around the playpen, hoisting themselves along with their wings, rather like babies just before they learn to crawl. The boiler was in the dining-room, which already smelled unacceptably ammoniac, and reluctantly I agreed with Nannie that there was no alternative to putting them in the old hen-house in a sunny corner of the garden, and letting them take their chance.

By evening, two had detached themselves from the huddle, and were staggering about in the sun, falling over and righting themselves, definitely more lively, though still pathetically weak. They made no attempt to escape when I approached to pick them up and shut them inside the house, but simply squatted to await their fate. Fear had been stamped out of them along with all other natural responses, and they would have done just the same had I been a fox.

Rehab was painfully slow, but day by day our little flock made progress towards becoming real hens again. Eight weeks after I brought them home, their missing feathers began to sprout as stubble, making them look even more unappetising than when they were naked. Egg production stopped abruptly after the first week, which was rather a blow, but instead of

looking at worms and insects with disgust, and ignoring all the leftover scraps from our table, they started to peck at the grass and make tentative efforts to scratch at loose soil.

We scooped out a shallow pit in their pen and filled it with mixed sand and ash, and a few days later it was a joy to see the most adventurous bird carefully lower herself into the dustbath, scuffling with evident pleasure and afterwards risking a rudimentary preen.

Perhaps the most surprising thing about these intensively reared, selectively bred, artificially housed automata was how quickly they developed individual personalities when living in natural conditions. One was bold and curious, a born leader of hens, and soon claimed her place at the top of the pecking order. As soon as they were let out in the morning, another would make a crazy dash for the wire-netting fence surrounding their run, and flutter against it as if trying to fly. They were quite noisy birds, but their clucking did not seem matched to the laying of eggs, as in normal hens – they just kept it up all the time. Pathetic as they were, they embodied something that had been lacking in our new home.

Their chance arrival reminded me strongly of the way my parents used to add all manner of waifs and strays to what they referred to as 'the strength'.

Whenever it was suggested that yet another hungry mouth of uncertain value, dubious provenance, and visibly down on its luck should be added to those already thronging their Radnorshire farm, my father and mother would exchange a look and a nod, and one would say. 'Well, why not? We'll put him (or her, or them) on the strength,' and with those words the newcomer or comers would acquire the right to a comfortable billet until death or some change of fortune removed him, her, or them.

I imagined the strength as a sort of infinitely expandable tent-cum-trampoline, impartially supporting and sheltering the motley crew that sought refuge there, making no distinction between those with two legs or four.

Among the human castaways taken on to it, I remember a morose submariner, who had unluckily developed claustrophobia. This so badly hampered his career that in desperation he turned his back on the sea and bought a run-down hill farm, which he had no idea how to manage. After a number of plagues, collapses, deaths and disasters, he turned to my parents for advice, and was taken on the strength until he should recover his equilibrium. Though he was gloomy company, seldom spoke and never joked, he did give me one piece of advice worth remembering. Never pick a fight on a submarine. I immediately assumed this was the cause of his troubles, and imagined him cowering in the bowels of the tiny vessel, deep in the dark water, trying to evade his enemy – but although his flirtation with agricultural life proved short-lived, it had a fairytale ending. About a year later, he met and married a clever, sensitive woman who owned a bookshop in Hereford; sold the farm, and left us to work as her business advisor.

Several war-widows were taken on the strength while they mopped their tears and readjusted to single life; and so were a succession of Antipodean cousins. The glowing-skinned girls stripped off at every opportunity to bask decoratively in whatever weak rays the Welsh sun provided, and made a very welcome distraction for passing tractor-drivers.

They threw themselves with enthusiasm into the social life of the Wye Valley, and one married a local lord, but the male visitors from Down Under were not so easy to please. They tended to be tough, spare, laconic young men with leathery complexions and eyes meshed in wrinkles from scanning the far blue yonder. They reckoned flocks and herds in thousands, and were dismissive of small-scale Welsh farming, hardly bothering to hide their contempt for people who called the vet when sheep were ill instead of simply cutting their throats. One went so far as to remark after a tour of the lambing-shed, 'Back home, all these would be culls,' a brutally frank assessment which greatly annoyed my mother.

On the strength, too, were foreign teenagers who hoped to improve their English, lovelorn South Africans getting over marital ructions, and the less-than-academic sons and daughters of friends whose parents had despaired of seeing them gainfully employed in dark suits in the City, or even of getting them into Agricultural College. However willing, they seldom had the temperament nor the necessary skills to be much use on the farm. Nevertheless they touchingly believed they were working for their keep, and the strength supported them uncomplainingly.

Four-legged refugees were made equally welcome, though their economic input was zero. In some cases it might even have been reckoned a costly burden, as when Shirley, who milked the cows and lived in a caravan, landed a promising living-in job in Worcestershire, only to find her prospective employer react with horror to the idea of accommodating Bonnie, her elderly Clumber spaniel.

In her frolicsome youth, Bonnie had probably deserved her name, but now her joints were stiff, her lower lids drooped, and a whiff of her long curly ears made you gasp. Shirley's choice was stark: she could take the job or the dog, but not both. 'Don't worry, we'll keep her here on the strength,' my father said equably when she broke the doleful news. So Bonnie lived out her remaining years stretched full length across the hearth-rug in front of the wood-burning stove, ensuring that everyone else sat in a whistling draught.

An even less rewarding dependent was Blacky, a heavy-crested superannuated part-Shire horse from a neighbouring farm, rescued on her way to the knacker. Though she would happily carry several children at once on her broad back, she resolutely declined any meaningful work either in chains, which would have been quite useful and taken the pressure off the little grey Fergie 20, nor would she pull either cart or gambo. She would stand like a rock to be harnessed, and backed willingly enough into the shafts, but thereafter neither clucking nor whipping would induce her to move. You could lead her a few paces, and then on went the brakes in the equine equivalent of a sit-down strike.

She took good care of herself though, did Blacky, in winter eating as much hay as three small ponies, and – worse – she seemed to be perpetually in season. Since she thought nothing of breaking through our admittedly rather straggly and fragile hedges in search of romance, much time and effort was spent either searching for her or blocking the resulting gaps – 'glatting' as it was known locally, and no one's favourite occupation. Despite this wilful refusal to recognise which side her bread was buttered, the strength supported Blacky for several years before she finally resumed her interrupted journey.

Then there was the bantam found sitting tight on her eggs in a load of straw, and a succession of unofficial dogs such as Joe, a skulking, shifty-eyed collie who had been turned out to live rough for some undisclosed crime, and was careful never to come within range of a stroking hand which might turn into a grabbing one. He would join in sheep-gathering operations on a freelance basis, and vanish again like a shadow, only returning to indent for rations when the other dogs were fed. His contemporary, Dawn, an emaciated pointer with a deformed jaw, was wished on my mother somehow, though she was a bag of nerves and useless on a grouse-moor; and another semi-permanent recruit to the strength was Bonzo, a canny, four-square, smooth-coated terrier who really belonged to the blacksmith, but would frequently put in an appearance at the witching hour of dog-dins.

No one grudged him his ration for, although not built for speed, Bonzo was an ace rabbiter. While the other dogs raced yapping in circles after their quarry, wasting energy and making a lot of noise, Bonzo would trot quietly to the exact point in the hedge where the rabbit planned to escape and wait patiently in ambush until he could chop it with a perfectly-timed pounce.

His rat-killing technique, too, was a marvel to behold. As the rick of oat-sheaves dwindled before the threshing machine, first a trickle and then a grey flood of fleeing rodents would pour out through the narrow gap between the barn door and the tractor whose belt was driving the machine. Positioning himself in the gap, like Horatius on the bridge, Bonzo would stand four-

square, flicking one rat after another over his shoulder in a slick, almost casual gesture that broke their necks with a single shake, leaving only the slimmest of pickings for any boy with a gun stationed beyond him.

Another dependent no one in their senses would have chosen was a beautiful, slinky, sealpoint Siamese queen whom Mummy saw dicing with death amid Hereford's market-day traffic.

When neither vets nor police could discover her owner, Marquesa (as we called her) was taken on the strength, and by sheer force of will soon evicted the resident cats from the farmhouse. Confident that her beauty and charm would always disarm criticism, she shamelessly exhibited all the faults for which Siamese are noted. As well as yowling constantly in a loud, complaining voice, she was a sneak-thief and bird-killer, a torturer of mice and shredder of loose covers, but the single act for which she is best remembered in the family was when she secretly, silently, gave birth to four kittens while sitting on the lap of a visitor watching television.

I liked my parents' open-handed acceptance of the principle that every waif and stray who asked for asylum should get it. While I was working in London and coming home only at odd weekends, I was hard put to it to catch up with news of the characters and foibles of the latest arrivals who had been added to the strength since my last visit, and when to my great delight my husband and I, together with our baby daughter, moved from our sixth-floor flat near Paddington to take on the lease of the handsome brick-and-flint farmhouse in the Chilterns where Duff had been brought up, my private plan was to gather animals – though not so many humans – round us in just the same way.

From the beginning, I recognised that it would have to be done on a smaller scale. Though the house was surrounded by a two-thousand-acre estate belonging to Duff's godfather, our own domain only stretched to the garden itself and perhaps an acre and a half of former orchard in front of the house, dominated by a couple of huge old Whiteheart cherry trees and a few dwarfish apples, dock-riddled and bisected by a rough farm track, a perfect starvation paddock for any pony prone to laminitis, but definitely not the place for valuable bloodstock.

The house was unusual in that the front door was seldom used. Though the building had clearly been designed to be approached uphill through the wood, across our paddock and through the garden to the front door, at some time in the past farming convenience had decreed that the back door should serve as the main entrance. This opened inward and took a bit of a push, putting you off-balance as you stumbled down two steps into a dark, dank bootroom floored with red flagstones, with a former wash-house dominated by a grim old copper for boiling laundry, but now used to store coal and firewood in separate bunkers on the left, and the door to the big, bare, brick-floored kitchen, with its old-fashioned, black, cast-iron cooking-range on your right. All through Duff's boyhood, he had ceremoniously lit this range at dawn on Christmas Day in order to roast the turkey, but I quickly decided this was one tradition ripe for breaking, and stuck to the electric oven. The extra-large, shallow Belfast sink, however, was useful for all sorts of purposes unconnected with the preparation of food. After hunting, you could dump saddlery in it until you felt strong enough to tackle the muddy leather, or scrub boots; you could wash sleeping-bags or a dog that had rolled in something noxious with equal ease – in short, it was an absolute treasure.

The kitchen was functional although far from cosy, but after this somewhat bleak approach to the house, it was an agreeable surprise to discover the large, well-proportioned rooms that made up the rest of it. Dining-room, library, nursery and sitting-room opened off a wide hall, with the garden door at one end in line with the original back door at the other, an arrangement which guaranteed maximum draughts whatever quarter the wind happened to be. Four big bedrooms plus a sliver of a dressing-room over the porch gave us plenty of space upstairs, and although there was only a single bathroom, two of the bedrooms were provided with basins.

I already knew the house well, indeed much of our courtship had been conducted in and around it, and when we married and my parents-in-law decided to go their separate ways, we jumped at the chance of taking on the lease of Bromsden Farm, which they had rented since before the war. Luckily for us, much of the large solid furniture with which the house was furnished was unsuited to either of their new homes and remained in situ to augment what we brought from London.

We moved on Grand National Day 1964, listening to the race as we slogged down the Cromwell Road through heavy rain and heavy traffic with our ten-month-old daughter Alice in the back of the car, under the watchful eye of the first person to be taken on to our own embryo strength, Nannie Barker. She had looked after Duff and his sister as small children, before they were taken to America when the second World War broke out in 1939, and had remained in touch with my mother-in-law throughout two decades and the raising of two other families.

Now, at the age of 60, she had qualified for and been offered a council flat in Stevenage, but her still-burning spirit of adventure made her reluctant to retire to its claustrophobic comfort, and she readily agreed to my suggestion that she should live with us and look after our children.

Any suggestion of pay she refused out of hand. 'I've never paid tax in my life, and don't want to start now,' she said briskly. 'I've got my pension, and that's enough for me.'

She was a trim, neat-figured little person with greying black curls and a round, guileless face, prominent exopthalmic eyes behind large, flamboyant, sparkly spectacles, tilted at the corners, and after a lifetime's experience she had a powerful rapport with babies and young children. The cooing, soothing, repetitious babble in which she communicated might drive strong men to drink, but it had a magical effect on small fry. Effectively she was a child-whisperer, capable of bringing even the naughtiest to heel without so much as raising her voice.

Born in 1904, the third girl in a family that eventually numbered twelve children, she had begun looking after her siblings at a tender age, and as soon as she left the village school was engaged to care for the children of the local doctor, whose wife was a byword for parsimony.

'Oh, but she was mean!' Nannie would recall. 'She used to scold me for spreading butter over the holes in the bread. When I told Mother about it on my day off, she took the loaf and she spread it with butter so thick you couldn't hardly see the crust. 'You eat that,' she said. 'I'll give her butter in the holes!''

Though we heard little about her father, her mother was constantly quoted and was clearly a remarkable woman,

keeping twelve children clean and fed, making sure they had
polished boots and clean pinnies for school and trooping them
off to Church every Sunday, all on the meagre wages of a farm
labourer during one of the worst periods for British agriculture
in the twentieth century.

Having lived through two World Wars herself, Nannie
knew everything there was to know about thrift, make-do-
and-mend, and the many ways to recycle leftovers. Any form
of profligacy or waste horrified her. She unravelled old jerseys
and from the wool created multi-coloured crochet blankets.
Her hands were always busy, making clothes for the children,
knitting sweaters, or creating new skins for semi-eviscerated
soft toys. She was a great believer in getting her charges out of
doors in all weathers, and gallantly pushed them in our smart
black London pram up and down the muddy lane as happily as
if it had been the smooth pavement of Kensington Gardens.

Although she must have been attractive as a young woman,
she had never married and was, I think, repelled by sex in all
its manifestations – though whether from some unfortunate
personal experience or simply having seen too much of the
result was never clear. She had a particular disparaging tone
when speaking about men in general and, while acknowledging
that they were necessary for the creation of her charges, one had
the impression that she regarded most of them as a poor feckless
lot. Certainly she much preferred the company and conversation
of children.

After spending so much of her life in other people's houses,
she was extremely good at fitting into different backgrounds
and routines, and so few, so firmly held were her prejudices that
we were careful to respect them. She would not, for instance, eat
in the kitchen, and joined us only for the meals we had in the
dining-room. She would not shop for food, had never driven a
car, and preferred to sup alone in the nursery with the television.
Nor did she like alcohol, which was just as well because the

merest sniff of sherry or ginger wine at Christmas went straight to her head.

We all considered it a happy coincidence that, although she was already drawing a pension, since her birthday fell on the 'missing day' – February 29th – when she joined us Nannie was still entitled to no more than 15 candles on her cake. Taking her on the strength was, as I quickly realised, the second-best spur-of-the-minute decision I ever made.

The farmhouse was surrounded on three sides by a garden, which had been extensively remodelled by my mother-in-law, when she began to live there permanently during the war. Determined to be as self-supporting as possible, she had turned a rectangle of former orchard below the house into a large vegetable patch surrounded by brick paths, skimming off the turf and digging compost into the unforgiving, flint-infested soil until it became productive enough to feed the household nearly all year round.

There was fruit, too. Two large Blenheim Orange trees with the washing-line strung between them provided all the apples anyone could eat and plenty over; there were, besides, gooseberry, blackcurrant and raspberries, a firmly-established rhubarb plant, and a carefully tended bed of strawberries, while an area of lawn stolen from the little paddock – and which I would have liked to return to it – supported a magnificent walnut tree.

Then there was also the original farm garden, a traditional long strip of lawn flanked by herbaceous borders full of (to me) unknown plants. Singlehandedly, my mother-in-law had dug and sown and reaped and mown, picked and stored and weeded and pruned for quarter of a century to keep this garden in good order, and the thought of the sheer physical effort it would take to maintain her standards made me feel quite faint.

Like most children, I had taken practically no interest in my parents' gardening efforts, and therefore had always been assigned boring, backbreaking jobs that required minimal skill. Weeding the drive just before visitors arrived was my particular bugbear.

Our England is a garden, and gardens are not made
By saying, 'Oh, how beautiful!' and sitting in the shade,
While better men than we go out and earn their
working lives
By grubbing weeds from gravel paths with broken
dinner knives,

I was never quite sure why Kipling considered these unfortunates better men than me, nor did I ever quite achieve the poet's triumphant apotheosis:

...When your back stops aching and your hands begin
to harden
You will find yourself a partner in the Glory of the
Garden

but there was a certain satisfaction in comparing the clean, uniform aspect of the completed stretch with the spotty, uneven look of the unweeded section, and the precise technique – the carefully calibrated pressure – needed to pull up a beastly little tuft of bittercress from its lair in the chippings without breaking off its long fragile root, remains embedded in my fingertips to this day.

Weeding gravel was, however, a pretty meagre preparation for the reality of managing our own garden, and Duff and I, together with the enthusiastic support of Nannie, embarked on a steep learning curve. Having the kiss of death on machinery, I was never entrusted with the mowing, nor did

Duff take much interest in the flowers, but the rest we tackled together, and despite inevitable mistakes – planting a peartree where the east wind shrivelled its blossom year after year, siting an expensive *hamamellis mollis* within reach of a grazing horse – the garden became, if not exactly a glory, at least a continuing pleasure.

Returning to the first recruits to our own strength, we fast forward a year to a heatwave the following May, and the former half-naked captives were hard to recognise. Glossy, full-feathered, red-combed and nimble, they scratched and pecked and scavenged like real chickens.

The great leap forward had followed the introduction of a bantam cock which a school-running neighbour found surplus to establishment. He was a stroppy, bossy, self-important little chap, very handsome; his body and wings a rich dark chestnut, with cape and tail-feathers shading into glossy black with green highlights. Having been chased and bullied by older, stronger birds in his youth, he now revelled in possessing his own little harem, and led the hens a merry dance, rounding them up and pointing out how delightful it was to peck at insects, kitchen scraps, worms, and all the other gourmet treats they had been deprived of in their youth.

He would hold out his wings, peacock-fashion, and stamp round some chosen belle, or give sudden chase to one he fancied treading. The meek, submissive hens found these bouts of lust very puzzling at first. They would crouch down the moment he began his run, and lie doggo until he had had his way with them, but by degrees I think they began to enjoy his attentions and became much sharper in their responses as they followed him about the run, copying whatever he did.

They even hopped up to the perches in the little henhouse

– no great height, but leaving the ground represented a great advance on their first months with us when they crouched on the floor at night. After a brief lay-off during the moult, eggs were fairly pouring out of them again: supersize eggs with smooth, delicately brown shells and yolks of the purest gold. We all agreed that the long months of TLC were being amply repaid.

The most tiresome hangover from their early career was their lack of time-sense. They would never retire voluntarily to their secure house at nightfall, but wait for some human to round them up, and as the days lengthened it became more and more difficult to remember to shut them up before predators made their nightly rounds. We knew there was at least one fox in close attendance because of the neat dropping with a cheekily twisted point which was often deposited by the gate to the run, and I suppose it was inevitable that sooner or later it would risk a raid.

When it came, though, it was not at night but in the middle of a hot afternoon, when I was playing with the children in the sandpit and Nannie upstairs having her post-prandial snooze. I had filled a watering-can and was sprinkling it to and fro while the children shrieked and dodged, when suddenly a different sound cut through their squeals – a harsh, squawking screech, cut short abruptly. We all spun round and stared.

'What's that?'

Nannie's head appeared at the bedroom window. 'Fox!' she cried, pointing towards the holly hedge. 'Look – over there!'

I dropped the water and sprinted towards the chicken-run, where a snowstorm of whitish-brown feathers was drifting idly across the beaten earth and piling up against the wire fence. As I wrenched open the gate not one but two small foxes, probably cubs, each with the limp body of a hen in its mouth, froze where they stood and regarded me coolly. Mounds of feathers marked where other victims had died, and choking rage boiled up in me. After all the months of rehabilitation, it seemed too cruel that these hapless birds should be casually beheaded by a pair of marauding teenagers, their lives snuffed out just when they had become worth living.

'Get out! Shoo!' I roared, snatching up flints from the path and throwing them as hard as I could.

Time to go, you could see one fox say to the other, and with unbelievable speed they melted away through the hole they had dug under the chicken-wire. A brief struggle as their feathered loot stuck in the gap, a few quick, expert tugs, and they were gone like shadows into the leafy shelter of the surrounding woods, leaving me to stare bleakly at the devastation they had wrought and brood on revenge.

It was a bitter end to our first experience of poultry-keeping but, as politicians remark after a catastrophe, lessons had been learnt, the first and most obvious being that foxes are bloody, bold, and resolute and hunt by day as well as by night, and the second that if chickenwire is expected to keep them out of the hen-run, it must be well dug in.

'With an overlap,' recommended the gamekeeper, who suffered from recurrent break-ins to his pheasant-rearing pens.

So before buying any more hens, we gave the entire run an upgrade, laying a foot width of chicken-wire flat to the ground along an encircling trench before replacing the turf and stapling it to six-foot uprights. Duff then strengthened the gate, putting solid boards on the bottom and sinking a stout railway sleeper into the ground to act as a fox-proof lintel. He replaced all the shaky tongue-and-groove boards in the hen-house itself, and put thick new rubberised felt over the pitched roof.

As one often finds when housing animals, the accommodation cost far more than the inmates. Once we began considering possibilities for break-*in* by fox rather than break-

out by hens, all sorts of security deficiencies became apparent. A branch overhanging the wire might provide a handy fox-ladder. It would have to go. The lid of the nesting-box was another vulnerable point. It could be pushed up by a questing nose and needed a strong catch. One by one the problems were identified and dealt with.

'Impregnable,' we agreed after several days' concentrated work, looking with satisfaction at the revamped run, and the following week I paid the first of many visits to the Domestic Fowl Trust in search of pure-bred birds.

So many breeds. So many gorgeous, extravagant feathered beauties. The difficulty was deciding which to choose. Though I knew in my heart that little meagre commercial hybrids ate less but laid far more reliably and far longer than ritzy purebreds, (and also that under my system of management they wouldn't remain pure-bred for long), I couldn't resist buying three proud, fluffy-footed, apricot Brahma hens and their tall consort, then adding a couple of slim, svelte Black Sumatra pullets, who looked as if they could outrun any fox, and a ridiculous Polish Chamois with pale grey plumage and the sort of hat worn by Audrey Hepburn in *My Fair Lady*'s Ascot scene.

Proof that the Henwife bug had bitten deep lay in the fact that I hardly blinked at the resulting bill. Even in the 'Sixties, each adult bird cost between £10 and £15 – a very considerable outlay – and it is not surprising that I drove them home with extreme care.

Installed in their new quarters, they began exploring at once, and showed none of the timidity of their predecessors. Indeed, they were thoroughly used to the crowds of humans who visited the Domestic Fowl Trust to peer into their individual runs, so to have the freedom of a large grassy pen with no wire underfoot suited them just fine. Grassy, that is, for about a month. Chickens – no matter how blue-blooded – have a unique propensity for creating squalor in their surroundings, and once

they had pecked and scratched the turf to mud, then excavated the driest parts of the run to create dustbaths, the whole area more closely resembled a mini Passchendaele than a gentleman's lawn. Moles added their mite to the destruction by throwing up heaps of fresh soil, and then – oh horror! – rats started to flock to the bonanza of kitchen scraps.

The first person to encounter a 'very big mouse' in the hen-house was the gently-nurtured three-year-old daughter of London friends, to whom I had offered the thrill of collecting eggs straight from the nesting-box. Though she wasn't shaken by finding a large, scaly-tailed rodent feasting on spilt yolk, I was. After yet another intensive bout of carpentry, the chicken run was beginning to look like Stalag Luft III, and as winter rain turned the bare soil to mud, the spectacular feathered feet which were the Brahmas' chief beauty, became sadly bedraggled.

Nothing for it, we decided, but to let them out completely. No more wire runs. No more clipping of flight-feathers. We would give them the freedom of garden and farmyard by day, shutting them up at night in a secure shed, and let them take their chance with foxes, dogs, heavy machinery, and all the other hazards inseparable from country living. We hoped that, although there would inevitably be accidents and losses, these would come singly rather than in battalions. Given a sporting chance to save themselves, the fittest would survive, adapting and breeding in true Darwinian fashion, and creating a flock of super-hens who could outsmart all their enemies.

That was the theory, and no one was more surprised than me when, broadly speaking, that was exactly what happened. It set the pattern for our poultry-keeping, wherever we happened to be living, for the next forty-five years.

As well as providing a more satisfying life for the flock, it was far more fun for us to see them *au naturel* – unconfined, busy about their complex affairs, constantly on the lookout for danger or for food, instinctively operating within a strict social hierarchy.

Top of the pecking-order in that first truly free-range flock was the stately Brahma cock we called Gandhi, who was quick and ruthless about punishing any younger male with ideas above his station. Even a reedy-voiced teenager who dared to crow too close to him received a vicious stab, which pulled out a clump of feathers. Attempting to seduce a hen merited a prolonged chase, which often ended with the would-be ravisher bloody about the comb.

Like all animals, chickens prefer the company of their own kind, and are acutely aware of differences between breeds. Next in influence and importance were the Brahma hens, always invited to be the first to partake of any delicacy while the old cock stood sentinel over them. The Black Sumatra hens he treated in an offhand, cavalier fashion, letting them eat only when his true wives had finished, and making it clear that although they belonged to his flock they were second-class citizens. When the inevitable inter-breeding between the races produced a generation of Black Sumatrans with feathery feet, he seemed to prefer them to their smooth-legged mothers. By then, though, there were several young cocks coming up through the ranks, and the old boy's supremacy was on the wane.

It was a sad day when I found him crouching in a clump of nettles, his head crusted with dried blood and defeat in his eyes. There must have been a titanic battle to reduce him to such a shadow of his pompous self, and though we patched him up physically, he never fully recovered his nerve.

I had feared that, free to roam where they pleased, the chickens might disappear into the surrounding beechwoods and be lost for ever, but in fact the little flock established its own boundaries, which extended no more than a hundred yards from the farmhouse in any direction, and their days quickly acquired a routine dictated by the position of the sun. They were constantly on the move, but their movements were predictable and I always knew where to find them.

As soon as the door of their shed was opened, they would hurry off to the sunniest corner of the Dutch barn, and for the next couple of hours you could be sure they would be hanging out there, feeding, quarrelling, preening, laying eggs, and loudly announcing that they had done so.

Then it would be time to seek shade and scuffle in dustbaths, something we sought to discourage in the vegetable garden, though with only limited success. Afternoon would find them perched on fences or the low branches of trees; as evening drew on they would visit the corn-hopper hanging from a beam outside the stables, and then when the light began to fade they would home in on their shed. One last drink, and they would flutter up to a favourite roost, make a few disobliging remarks to whoever was next in line, and by dusk they would be settled for the night, so all we had to do was slam and bolt the door.

Another pleasure – particularly for a household with children – is seeing the way chickens dispose of table scraps.

Apart from lettuce, oranges and olives, nothing is too exotic for them to enjoy. Curry is a particular favourite, a reminder of their Asiatic roots, and leftover pasta or stale cake sends them into a frenzy of delight.

Though we tried to keep track of their nests and always had plenty of eggs for the house, we must have missed hundreds along the way. Whenever I found a nest containing more than seven or eight, it seemed prudent to drop them in a bowl of water to test their freshness. Discovering an embryo chick in the eggs one is about to scramble is a sure way to kill one's appetite. On one occasion Duff invited a gang of visiting children to collect all they could find in the straw bales stacked up high in the Dutch barn, offering a rate of sixpence per egg. Great was his consternation when the search-party returned, covered in bits of straw, with 180 eggs, some of them very old indeed, in their plastic buckets.

Every so often, a hen would secretly build up a clutch in some hidden corner and settled down to brood them. At first, when I became aware of this, I used to wait until dark and then carefully transfer her into a secure coop, but only the most docile hens would tolerate this treatment. Most of them would start to stamp about and rage at their confinement, smashing their eggs in the process. It was, I found, better not to interfere, and let them take their chance. During the three weeks when she is using all her heat and energy to incubate her eggs, a hen – or any sitting bird – gives off so little scent that a predator can pass close by without winding her.

In the warmest part of the day, when she senses that her nest will not chill for half an hour, she will leave it briefly while she forages, drinks, and fluffs up her feathers. Hurrying about with ruffled plumes and an air of preoccupation, brusquely repelling any attempt at fraternisation by the cock, pecking frantically at corn as she tanks up for the next session of sitting, her demeanour is unmistakably that of a harassed mother-to-be, and during these short forays I would be able to inspect the nest, remove obviously addled eggs, and sprinkle water to dampen the remaining ones. This gives the hatchling a better chance of breaking out of the shell, particularly if the hen has chosen a dry spot among haybales or on top of a wall. Standing there in the quiet of the barn, I would hear the tiny *chip-chip* of egg-teeth – the prominent hook on the beak which Nature provides as a hammer – as the chicks tapped away at their prison, but despite the powerful temptation to take a peek at what was going on under the feathers, it was vital to leave well alone until the hen herself decided to give her family a look at the world.

The hatching process might take forty-eight hours if several different hens had contributed to the nest. It was tantalising to catch a glimpse of fluff as the first cheeper moved within the cocoon of feathers, but – as I eventually learned – the iron rule was No Interference.

In the early days, worried that the first-hatchers might be hungry or thirsty, I tried putting a saucer of water or a few chick-crumbs within reach, but it was always a mistake. Either the hen would reach out to peck the food, crushing any egg still in the process of hatching, or a new chick would topple into the water and get chilled. Having satisfied her appetite, the hen would not be spurred by hunger-pangs into leaving the nest at the right moment.

One way and another it was much better to let well alone.

When she did eventually sally forth from the messy, dishevelled nest, she let everyone know the extent of her triumph. Clucking continuously, with legs bent and wings held out like an umbrella, the new mother would usher the tiny balls of fluff into the open, carefully shielding them from wind and rain, and attacking with the utmost ferocity anyone who took too close an interest. In some warm, sheltered spot, she would gather the chicks round and begin to demonstrate vital life-skills.

Scratching. Pecking the soil. Dipping miniscule beaks into water and raising their heads to let it trickle down their throats. While they were thus engaged, I would put on rubber gloves and hastily clear out the abandoned nest, removing broken shells, soiled bedding and unhatched eggs. These burst like miniature grenades, releasing a really horrible smell, but it was imperative to break them, preferably by throwing them against a tree, because if left intact they would lie in the muck-heap for months, the smell getting worse all the time, until eventually someone trod on them.

Many and varied are the survival instincts programmed into the chicks from the moment they hatch. With a single warning cluck, soft and guttural, the hen can silence their incessant cheeping and freeze them into immobility while she waits for danger to pass. Family discipline is tight. If the menacing shadow of a crow or buzzard appears overhead, or a domestic predator – dog, cat, or human – comes too close, she will attack with reckless valour. Even horses and cows retreat hurriedly, their body-language saying, 'Sor-*ree!* My mistake,' in the face of an onslaught by a furious, fluffed-up mother hen.

Her colleagues also give her a wide berth while the chicks are tiny. The bold, bossy, bullying cocks stand back humbly while she feeds, and other hens move away if she shows an inclination to scratch in a particular spot.

Though she will defend her chicks to the death, a hen's charity does not extend to youngsters from another brood – rather the reverse. Once I had two clutches hatch on consecutive days, but when both sets of chicks were barely a week old, one of the mothers was killed by a dog. I collected up four tiny orphans who had hidden in the nettles, and when darkness fell I pushed them underneath the surviving hen in a secure coop. She moved her feathers to accommodate the newcomers, and settled back with the augmented brood, and I tiptoed away, thinking that come morning she wouldn't be able to distinguished between her own offspring and the interlopers.

My mistake.

As soon as I opened the coop in the sunlight, the adoptive mother gave a loud squawk, sprang in the air, and beat her wings wildly, terrifying all the chicks, which scattered and hid. Then with soft, confidential clucks, she called them towards her, but only her own family recognised her voice and ran to her, while the orphans fled still farther away. Solomon himself couldn't have devised a neater way of establishing their true parentage.

For the best part of a month, hen and chicks remain close together, scuttling here and there, pecking and scratching, sleeping as a single unit. Then, gradually they drift apart. As the chicks' downy fluff is replaced by proper feathers, instinct tells them that safety lies in height, leading them to perch on any handy rail or branch, while the hen's periods of brooding them on the ground become correspondingly shorter.

They start to scorn the safety of the coop, perching in a rebellious row on its ridge, refusing to go in unless caught by hand. Few jobs are more frustrating and time-consuming than trying to entrap lively chicks as dusk falls, and at this point I am inclined to throw in the towel, herd them into the shed with the adult birds, and hope they survive attacks by rats or their curmudgeonly seniors. Some do and some don't. Unless you accept at the outset that Nature provides far more chicks than you can expect to grow to maturity, free-range poultry-keeping is not for you.

Still, I admit it is harrowing to listen to the desperate cries of chicks when their mother flies cheerfully up to a perch they cannot reach, and stamps about, peering down and calling them to join her. Again and again they flutter as high as they can, only to fall back, defeated.

One answer is to prop a stepladder against the beam and encourage the chicks to hop up, rung by rung; but it could be argued that this is taking TLC too far. The fact is that, left alone, the hen will solve the dilemma in one of two ways. Either she will accept that she has jumped the gun, and fly down to brood her family on the floor, or the little things will find a perch halfway up, where she will finally join them, expertly tucking them under her wings and silencing the cheeping for the next eight or nine hours.

For a few more weeks this happy arrangement continues, and then one day – quite abruptly, without warning – the hen severs the family connection. Off she goes to start laying again and fraternising with the rest of the flock, and drives away the half-grown chicks if they try to make a claim on her. It is as if she is saying, 'Right. I've taught you all I can. Now you're on your own.'

Curiously enough, given their suffocating closeness up to that point, the youngsters accept this change in their circumstances with very little protest. The strongest will appoint himself leader, and for about three months the little band will behave very much like human teenagers. They hang about on the fringes of society, refuse to go to bed until very late and, in the case of the reedy-voiced cockerels, make themselves a thorough nuisance, harassing elderly females with improper suggestions and sparring noisily.

How those young cocks love fighting! Anything or everything will set them off, ruffling neck feathers, raising and lowering their beaks in a duellist's salute, and then suddenly springing together with raking spurs and buffeting wings. The more evenly matched they are, the worse the conflict. They go at it hammer and tongs until one of the combatants turns tail and runs. Even then he may think better of it and swing round for another bout, but despite all the sound and fury these are only practice fights, and it is rare for a youngster to be seriously injured.

When mature cocks do battle it is another story. You can see that they actually want to kill one another, and once defeated even the most vainglorious supremacist becomes a craven shadow of his former self. The weakness of their vanquished lord is ruthlessly emphasised by his wives, who scold and peck him, for kicking a man when he is down is a favourite sport among poultry. When I asked Duff to shoot one ancient cock with a .22, instead of going through the hassle of catching and executing him, the old bird collapsed with a squawk, stone dead, and in an instant all his mates set on the corpse, stamping and pecking with distressing ferocity, as if they had been waiting for this opportunity for months. *Vae victis.*

Brutal as it sounds, putting an abrupt full stop to an ailing bird is often the kindest thing to do. Besides, it minimises the risk of some bug spreading through the flock. When you notice the feathers around a bird's vent clogged up with whitish discharge, the sensible thing is to cull it at once. Coccidiosis is a common culprit, but there are many strains. Testing a sample of faeces and treating with the appropriate antibiotic is a waste of time and money, because even if the bird recovers it is unlikely to lay again.

The same goes for the lordly Cock of the Walk, when he is beaten in fair fight. His body may heal, but his spirit is broken, and all the other birds know it. For a week or two he may skulk furtively on the outskirts of the flock, but it is only a matter of time before he fails to make it to the shelter of the shed at night, and by morning there will be just a drift of feathers to mark his passing.

Chicks face so many hazards in their first days of life that no more than a quarter are likely to reach maturity. That said, I have known some astonishing survivals against the odds, as in the case of a day-old chick, separated from its siblings during a thunderstorm, who failed to reappear when the sun came out and the hen summoned her brood together, yet we knew it must be alive, because we could hear it cheeping.

Like human babies, chicks have disproportionately loud

voices, and we scoured every inch of the covered yard, trying to locate the frantic *peep-peep-peep* that seemed to be coming from anywhere and everywhere. It was nearly dark and the sound was growing weak when our daughter, Alice, shone a torch through the grille of a storm-drain, and spotted the chick some eighteen inches below ground, balanced on a couple of straws, in imminent peril of being washed down the pipe.

That was a very lucky escape. More often you see the family dwindle gradually, as one chick after another meets its fate, but as my mother used to say bracingly, if they all survived, the world would be taken over by chickens, and who wants that?

CHAPTER TWO

First Friends

A dog is for life, not just for Christmas warn the car-stickers, and quite right too. Fourteen or fifteen long years may well separate the adorable playful puppy from the creaky, cranky ruin for whom death is the most merciful option, and during every moment of those years the owner is responsible for that dog. He must feed it, shelter it, train, restrain, and entertain it. He must always know where it is and what it is doing. And when that dog's life becomes a burden, he alone must make the decision to end it.

Thinking of it like that makes your blood run cold. '*Quelle servitude!*' as a French cousin once remarked (though in his case the pet in question was a – fairly – tame wild boar.) Even with dogs, though, it follows that anyone with his head screwed on will think long and hard before acquiring a puppy, consider the merits and drawbacks of every breed, its suitability for whatever purpose he has in mind, and whether it will fit in with family life. Once he has settled on a particular breed, he will surely take care to research pedigrees and background, visit breeders and follow up advertisements in search of the ideal animal.

Since we knew all this perfectly well, in retrospect it seems strange that the first dog we took on the strength was foisted on us in much the same way that so many animals had joined my parents' household. Young, well-bred, but surplus to requirement as she was, there could be no question of rejecting Kate, the black labrador, when her owner died; nor was his death a surprise since, on the very first occasion he met my husband, Ron had announced in an abrupt, confrontational tone that forbade commiseration, that he had cancer and was living on borrowed time.

An aggressive, terrier-like man with a wiry pepper-and-salt beard, he drove up to our house unannounced one Spring morning with the half-grown black bitch in the back of his Mini estate, and more or less demanded that Duff should take him stalking deer in the surrounding woods until he became too weak to shoot.

'And when I die, I want you to take my dog,' he said flatly.

It is difficult to refuse a man who is under sentence of death, and Duff agreed to both propositions (though he didn't tell me about the second at the time.)

While I am not exactly anti-dog, I prefer them to live outside and have never understood why people feel the need to share their homes with these particular small carnivores, whose housekeeping habits conflict in every way with those of humans. Dogs have many talents and uses, but as housemates they suck. Only rigorous training and continual discipline prevents them from turning your home into their kennel, and neither training nor disciplining has ever been my strong suit.

Take the most obvious area of conflict: food. His magnificent sense of smell tells a dog exactly what is on the humans' table, and it would be idle to suppose that he would not prefer a shoulder of lamb to the miserable chunks of mixed cereal and soya in his own feed-bowl. Yet his perfectly understandable attempt to exchange one for the other brings a torrent of abuse, if not blows and curses – so unfair when he is simply following his instinct. But at the same time as denying him our own food, we prevent him from scavenging for all the delicacies dogs enjoy and we do not. Carrion. Dung. The contents of dustbins. Rancid curds dropped by lactating cows. And so on.

Then there is the vexed question of the particular space

within the house which he can call his own. Given the choice, a dog will opt for an armchair, well-upholstered sofa or even a box-spring mattress well above floor-level draughts, and to this he will naturally gravitate despite his owner's vigilance, even when he has been taught to lie in a basket on the ground. Even in his own home, jumping on furniture is generally forbidden, and absolutely taboo in other people's houses; nor must he relieve himself on the carpet, bury bones beneath the sofa cushions, or chew rugs and chair-legs.

Outside the house he may not bite strangers, chase sheep or cats, dig up flowerbeds, bark at postmen, snap at children, eat cowpats or roll in badger droppings. He may not scratch at fleas or lick his privates in company, fight, chase bitches, pheasants or livestock.

The list of no-nos is never-ending, and nearly as restrictive are the things he must do to order, though few if any come naturally to him. Walking at heel. Sitting and staying. Keeping still and quiet while guns blast off close to him. Picking up dead game and delivering them to his handler without taking so much as a bite for himself. Coming back when called, even if the scent of a hot bitch or a catchable rabbit is burning his nose, drawing him like a powerful magnet, and his owner's voice is faint in his ears. And he must travel in the luggage space of a smelly, noisy, metal box on wheels, and remain incarcerated there, sweltering or shivering according to season, until his master at last returns to the vehicle.

Hardly the existence Man should wish on his best friend, but that's what a dog's life boils down to, and because so little of what he is allowed to do comes naturally, a battle of wills is inevitable – a battle which I invariably lose. Does it really matter? I think when the dog disobeys a direct order, and because he senses my uncertainty, he instantly decides: *No, it doesn't.*

Look at good dog-trainers and you see at once that uncertainty never enters their minds. They have a particular tone of voice – sharp, minatory, hard-edged – which commands canine attention. Strong, confident and focused, they know exactly how to dominate, exploiting their dog's inbuilt desire to keep in with the leader of the pack. In fact, to train dogs successfully you have to *become* the leader of the pack, endlessly dominant, utterly consistent. You are the boss, and neither of you must forget it for a moment. You mustn't allow the dog to go through a door ahead of you, you must not lie on the ground so he can look down on you. You must reward obedience and punish rebellion instantly, just as a pack-leader does, and your dog will understand the rules because that is the way canine society is ordered.

Knowing how to treat a dog is one thing but putting the knowledge into practice quite another. I have never been a pack leader, finding the whole business of being the boss mentally exhausting. And this is no doubt why, within a few months of Kate's arrival with us, her standards of behaviour had slipped noticeably. Ron had confounded medical opinion by living another two years after his first appearance at our house, so Kate was fully grown – a quiet, meek, short-coupled labrador with a charmingly broad domed head and sleek short coat, a broad otter-tail, and the sort of figure that easily spreads.

Too quiet, she seemed to me. Too biddable, in fact verging on the lethargic, and in an effort to cheer her up I relaxed many of the strict rules she had been trained to respect. At first she looked amazed when incited to jump on to the wide sofa which took up most of one wall of Duff's study, and when she eventually crept on to it she looked the picture of guilt: with bent legs and drooping ears, she curled up very small in the farthest corner and kept completely still.

A month later, however, and she was sprawling at her ease, paws stretched out fore and aft, even raising her hackles if another animal looked like joining her – such a fixture on the sofa that any human who wanted to sit there had difficulty inducing her to budge up and make room. I also found it hard to resist the interest she showed in my cooking. It was undeniably convenient to have an eager scullery-maid who would clean the roasting tin right down to the shiny metal: she saved me a fortune in Brillo pads. She would rapidly hoover up any foodstuff from the floor, and edge-of-plate scraps rejected by the children found an appreciative consumer. So great was the appeal in her big brown lollipop eyes, so charming the gently-waving tail as she sat right beside one's chair, that the temptation to slip her bits off the plate was almost overwhelming.

Inevitably her figure, which had always been comfortable, began to balloon, for despite all the exercise she took on her sporting expeditions, around the house she was extremely indolent and often remained in the same place for hours on end. I was surprised, too, to find how much the presence of a single labrador added to the housework. Quite apart from large, muddy pawprints on the kitchen floor's tiles, her black coat was continually shedding, not just in the normal seasonal changes of spring and autumn, but all year round.

When it began to come out in handfuls, I was alarmed enough to arrange a blood test. It revealed an under-performing thyroid gland, which explained not only her bulging eyes but also her habitual lethargy. The vet gave her pills, but these came too late to prevent her entire coat falling out. Few creatures look more repellent than a fat, bald labrador with a grey, wrinkled skin and I am sure poor Kate felt it keenly. Though the vet assured us it was nothing catching, her unnatural appearance made people disinclined to touch her, as they would have shrunk from a leper. No one was more relieved than me when at last a faint fuzz began to cover her nakedness, but it was a good six months before she looked normal again.

Kate was nearly four when we woke up with a jolt to the fact that if we wanted to breed from her, it was now or never. In fact she was already rather old for a prima gravida, but since she had been full-grown when we had took her on, we had nearly forgotten that her breeding window was rapidly closing. Once a bitch has had one litter, and proved that all systems are in working order, she can go on breeding merrily into old age – my mother's labrador produced four puppies when she was ten years old – though obviously the process is riskier for an elderly bitch, and the Kennel Club declines to register puppies born to mothers over eight.

The hunt began at once for a suitable sire, one who would complement Kate's looks and character and minimise those aspects in which she was less than perfect, in particular the malfunctioning thyroid. A well-bred energetic dog with a good thick coat and a host of distinguished ancestors was what we had in mind, and pretty soon we found what appeared an ideal partner, Goldcoin by name, a proven stud dog with the coveted Ch for Champion liberally scattered throughout his pedigree, of charming looks and nature, and living a mere thirty miles away.

Kate duly came in season, a date was arranged, and the mating took place with never a hitch. Very soon it was apparent that she was pregnant, and we waited with bated breath for the happy event.

What we had failed to take into account, however, was that we would have been better suited by a *working* labrador sire rather than one bred for the show-bench. Even working labradors fall into two categories, the so-called Peg Dog which traditionally belongs to a Gun – usually a large-boned retriever with a noble head who is required to sit quietly at his master's peg throughout each drive, and only pick up the birds he has shot when the horn has blown and the guns fall silent – and the Keeper's Dog – generally sharper, lighter and more athletic in build and distinctly more energetic – who hunts through the coverts in the beating line, driving game towards the guns.

Show labradors, on the other hand, are bred less for sporting use than for their looks and sunny natures. All the built-in physical characteristics of the breed are slightly exaggerated. Their noses are shorter, their foreheads and chests broader, their coats thicker. They are generally more rounded in figure than either of the working types, and must be placid enough to wait for their classes for hours, sit on a bench, submit to endless grooming, and look happy when obliged to pose with their tails humiliatingly stretched out by their handlers.

Goldcoin – aka Barney – belonged in the show-dog category. He had never been trained to retrieve game, and though friendly and extrovert by nature as well as being undeniably handsome with his rich, thick yellow coat, short broad head, and blunt tail, he was at heart a pet rather than a *compagnon de chasse,* lacking the special skills needed by sporting dogs: their drive and stamina, unquestioning obedience, the hunting instinct hardwired into the depths of their being. Kate herself, though bred on the same lines, had never been near the show-ring and was a fanatically keen hunter. A better choice of sire to complement her bloodline would have been a Field Trial Champion, but with her about to give birth it was too late for second thoughts.

The long-expected day came, and passed, and nothing happened. Two more crawled by, with Kate becoming balloon-like and more lethargic by the hour, and then one wet evening when we had almost forgotten her condition and were about to go to bed, she lumbered off the sofa and asked to go outside.

I opened the back door and saw her pad off towards the lilac bush on the edge of the little pond and, when I called her a few minutes later for her bedtime biscuit, she hurried back indoors shaking water from her coat, and heaved herself back on the sofa.

No action tonight, we thought; but seeing she was already overdue we decided to take turns in checking her at four hourly intervals. It seemed that I had barely fallen asleep before Duff was shaking me awake again, saying, 'She's had two puppies,' and sure enough, there was Kate looking very pleased with herself, whining softly as she licked and nuzzled the rolypoly little slugs, one yellow, one black, the picture of fulfilled motherhood.

And that, it seemed, was that. Labradors are noted for large litters, and the vet had told us to expect four puppies at least, but everything in Kate's demeanour suggested she considered the incident closed. No huffing or straining or panting: all she seemed to yearn for was a good long sleep. The puppies didn't look particularly big, but after waiting for two hours we decided she wasn't going to produce any more, so we arranged a barrier of chairbacks and cushions to stop them falling on to the floor, gave Kate a fresh bowl of water, and went back to bed.

Next morning brought a sad explanation. Two dead puppies, sodden with rain, lay in the garden, one under the lilac bush and the other on the concrete path – a sharp lesson never to allow an overdue bitch out alone, particularly in the dark. Still, Kate buckled down to motherhood with great enthusiasm and the little survivors grew exponentially on rations designed for four.

From the sofa where they were born, they moved to a comfortably secluded, curtained lair in the lower half of one kitchen cupboard, which we had adapted to serve as a whelping box, and for the next three weeks it was easy to forget they were there, so quietly did the sleek little butterballs sleep and feed, feed and sleep in their dark cave, so discreetly did their mother pop in and out to attend to them. It was a happy, tranquil, easygoing period: the calm before the storm.

The first indication that calm had run its course was when I glanced down and met the gaze of bright eyes peering out from beneath their curtain. Next morning four front paws were reaching for the top of the confining plank, and hours later a fat body hoisted itself ponderously on to the edge, swayed back and forth, and plopped like a jellyfish on to the lino. Hastily I put it back where it belonged, but that was it: once one had the trick, the other followed. By lunchtime it was plain that kitchen days were over.

Time to move to the outdoor kennel, but now the weather, which had been exceptionally warm for April, turned wet, cold and windy. We screened the front of the kennel with a builders' sheet to cut down the draught and, though it was distinctly colder than the kitchen, cuddled together in the carpeted inner house the puppies were cosy enough.

Now the pace of their development hotted up. Hardly had we learnt to cope with one stage than they were on to the next. Worming at weekly intervals. Solid food to take the strain off Kate, who was beginning to look gaunt and ragged although she was eating wolfishly. Since this was before the days of specially-balanced puppy-feed containing all essential nutrients, vitamins, minerals and so on, we gave them raw beef mince mixed first with Farex (in which they dabbled their paws and spread all over the newspaper on which we had placed the bowl), then with bashed-up dog-biscuit.

By now Kate was getting pretty fed up with their demands, and visited them only briefly before hopping out of the kennel with a martyred look. We gave them playtime for twenty minutes or so morning and evening and this, together with feeding and cleaning out the kennel, took sizeable chunks out of our waking hours as the puppies grew more athletic and adventurous. Their energy would seem inexhaustible until they returned to the kennel to crash out in a gently twitching dog-pudding; inexhaustible, too, was their goodwill towards people.

They learnt to come to a whistle and a reward of mince, and perfected less admirable skills like rolling in muck, tearing clumps of lupins to shreds, and open-cast mining on the lawn. Chickens squawked and fled at their approach, the horses trod warily, careful not to step on soft paws. The cats eyed them coldly and stood their ground with fur fluffed out and tails bent in menacing arches until the puppies retreated abashed, ears drooping.

Meanwhile, we were coping with paperwork and the vaccinations puppies need before they leave home or mix with other dogs. Forms flew back and forth from the Kennel Club and eventually we were issued with an eight-generation pedigree for each of them. Since there were only two we were spared the worry of choosing new owners. The spherical black bitch we called Pumpkin and planned to keep, while Buie – the yellow dog who looked so like his father – was going to live with him in part payment of the stud fee.

All our subsequent ventures into breeding labradors have, with minor variations, followed very much the same pattern – a month of peace followed by four weeks of intense activity – but the real difference has been that in every other case the litters have been much larger, and at the age of eight weeks most of the puppies had to be sold. Eight from Pumpkin's first litter of nine. Seven from her second, and seven again – all of whom we sold – from an unauthorised misalliance with an Irish sheepdog. Pumpkin's daughter Pansy produced seven, eight, and eleven puppies and Jemima, a black bitch from a different family when Kate's line came to an end, produced first nine and then a whopping twelve, far too many for her to cope with alone.

Even when we and Nature had reduced the litter to a manageable size, they meant continual hard work for us all, plus an anxious fortnight while we assessed the characters and capabilities of people who replied to advertisements. There is a critical moment in a puppy's development, between the age of eight and ten weeks, when it is weaned by its dam and needs to bond anew, preferably with a human, and any delay makes the process harder and the relationship less secure.

When the advertisements appeared in the sporting and local press, the telephone would begin to ring and keep it up intermittently for several months – long after all the puppies were placed – as people read back numbers of the magazine and were seized with a desire for a young labrador. But how can you tell from a half-hour visit whether a total stranger is a suitable owner for your puppy?

We made some ground rules. Callers who asked if the dog would be all right on his own while they were out at work all day we dismissed out of hand, and we were wary of those who said their children longed for a puppy, but even with those caveats it was difficult to choose between prospective buyers.

They were all so different. Sometimes the wife called the shots and sometimes the dog-lover was plainly the husband. Some brought 'expert' friends who clapped loudly in the astonished puppies' faces and gave them psychological tests. Others clasped them to their bosoms and shrieked when their faces were licked. Some were keen on bloodlines and assiduously perused pedigrees and hip/eye scores, but many prospective owners barely glanced at the papers. Some asked the price and held whispered consultations; others simply reached into their back pockets.

One sturdy black dog puppy was bought and paid for in minutes by a local woman who seemed both knowledgeable and sensible, only for her to bring him back next morning saying shamefacedly that her four-year-old son was terrified of him. Another dog from the same litter we saw driven away with deep misgiving because although the husband wanted him, the wife, who would be in charge of him during office hours, was tepid-to-cool about having a dog at all. She would have preferred a bitch, fearing that a dog might lift his leg against her yew hedges, but since all the bitches were already spoken for, it was the dog or nothing.

We worried a good deal about that puppy – needlessly as it turned out, for when we saw him a year later he was plainly the pride of the family, tall, handsome, and completely at one with his owners. What's more, the yew hedges had survived unscathed.

At ten weeks, when all his siblings had been sold, a single yellow dog puppy remained from Jemima's second litter and, inconveniently, I had lost my heart to him. Not a good choice. He was a low-slung, rather serious little chap, always half a beat behind the others. The wrong colour for deer-stalking, the wrong sex for a bitch-owning household, but I loved him, weaving fantasies of a non-sporting companion who would help with the sheep and poultry and scorn the pursuit of game.

It was not to be. At the eleventh hour a large, jolly Indian lady, a professional carer, swept into the yard and scooped him into her arms. Even I could see they were made for one another. Spreading sweetness and light among the sick and elderly was just what this puppy would do best. As her big 4x4 drove away, his solemn yellow face and ears just visible above the dashboard, we could only wish him – along with the rest of the litter – all the luck in the world, because he was sure to need it.

Try as the breeder may to give each puppy he sells the best possible chance, there is no ducking the fact that a dog's life is a lottery. Once they leave home you are unlikely ever to see them again, and you have no control over the circumstances in which they will spend the next fifteen-odd years. With hindsight, I see we were lucky that Kate's first litter presented us with no problems of ownership at all.

Kate and Pumpkin, Pumpkin and Pansy, Pansy and Zephyr – we continued with mother-and-daughter partnerships through several generations, always retaining one female descendant of Kate's until that particular line came to a halt with Zephyr who, despite repeated attempts, failed to breed. But though the female line had remained constant, a different sires had produced large variations in their looks and temperament.

Show-bred on both sides, Pumpkin was as round as her name implies, but when we chose as her mate a lean, rangy

Field Trial Champion, the resulting puppies were slim and long-legged, twice as fast as their dam and, it has to be said, far from biddable. Pansy could run down a rabbit and would course a wounded pheasant over several fields before shouts and whistles recalled her to a sense of her duty. Even when held at the peg by a choke lead, she could burst my fingers open with a violent heave if she saw the chance of leaping at a low-flying bird, and by no stretch of imagination could she be called a good gun-dog.

As a deerstalker's helpmeet, however, she came into her own, creeping silently behind Duff as he padded through the woods at dawn and dusk, ready to freeze to immobility when he put out a warning hand, and drop to the ground at the faintest hiss. He could leave her sitting, tense as a wire spring, while he crawled forward into a firing position, and if by chance temptation overcame her and she wriggled forward to join him, it was in absolute silence.

She never had the least difficulty in distinguishing between her two roles, and automatically adjusted her behaviour according to whether he was carrying a rifle or a shotgun. The faintest jingle of the keys to the gun cupboard had her out of her basket in a trice, huffing and wiggling and thrashing her tail with delight at the prospect of sporting action. Though a black dog shows up very clearly against the soft greys and greens of hills when stalking red deer in Scotland, she was so low to the ground that providing she stayed to heel, the legs of the stalkers in front concealed her until they actually moved on to their firing point, when she had to be put on the lead and held a few yards back for fear of inadvertently spooking an out-lying deer. Her reward for silence and stillness was permission to supervise the gralloch and possibly solicit a morsel of liver.

It was when stalking fallow deer in leafy woodland, however, that she was invaluable. Shot through the heart, a beast will frequently make a great leap forward, and all too easily vanish in some small hollow full of thick brambles or scrub. Off

Pansy would shoot off like an arrow, nose glued to the blood-spoor, and bay the dead beast until her master came up.

With each of our labradors in turn, I would be surprised by the way in which so gentle a house-dog would be transformed into a fearless hunter who had no hesitation in tackling a quarry many times her size, and my heart was in my mouth on one occasion in Scotland when I was left in charge of cobby, short-legged Jemima, while Duff crawled forward for the last hundred yards.

We of the rearguard settled down to wait silently among the peat-hags, tucking hands into pockets in search of warmth, and had been dozing fitfully for twenty minutes or so when startled into full alertness by the shot. Jemima sat up, tense as a spring, while we waited for a signal that all was well, and when it eventually came I released her to join her master a couple of hundred yards ahead.

Prematurely, as it turned out. Though the stag had crumpled and vanished into the network of hags, he was by no means dead, and as the men walked forward peering to right and left, he suddenly appeared between them and the dog.

Jemima, who had been making a beeline for her master, swerved and hurtled directly towards the stag, which swung to face her, head lowered, antlers as menacing as a *cheval de frise*. For a moment they confronted each other in classic pose no more than six feet apart, the stout little black bitch with lips drawn back and teeth bared, ears flat to her head, and the stag daring her to come on.

We humans stood frozen in horror, the rearguard too far away to intervene, the stalkers themselves too close to shoot without endangering the dog. In any case no shout or whistle would have penetrated Jemima's concentration and, with those wickedly sharp antlers so close, any distraction might have proved fatal.

Wild-dog instinct was closer to the surface than I imagined, though, and as the stag stamped, breaking the spell, Jemima circled behind him to nip and worry as expertly as if she had rehearsed this scenario a dozen times. Round jumped the stag, antlers thrashing. Round darted Jemima, evading by a whisker the branching spikes seeking to impale her. For a moment more the deadly dance continued until suddenly the stag had had enough.

Away he cantered, with Jemima pursuing close enough to bring him to bay once more, but her short legs were no match for his great bounds, and as the space between them increased, the stalker took a snap neck-shot and the stag crumpled in the heather.

My mouth was dry and my heart racing as if I had run a mile as I rushed to put the fearless hunter back on the lead. Never again, I vowed. Never again will I put her in such danger. But danger comes in unexpected forms, and unfortunately it was a promise I was unable to keep.

In common with many thick-coated dogs, outdoor living suits labradors best and Jemima was always perfectly comfortable sleeping in the kennel just across the farmyard from our bedroom window. From her miniature four poster bed she could monitor the comings and goings of badgers, foxes, cats and other nocturnal prowlers. She knew exactly when the household began to stir: first the radio, then the bedroom light, bathroom light, then the clump of feet on the stairs, and could gauge to a second how long it would take between the rattle of curtains drawn back to the turning of the porch key as the first riser came to let her out.

Sometimes as I dressed I would watch her uncurl from her tight, Chelsea-bunlike sleeping position with tail covering nose, stretch, yawn, bow, then sit up straight with ears pricked as the familiar household sounds succeeded one another, her tail wagging ever more furiously as the moment of release approached. A few joyful licks and paws-ups, a couple of laps of the yard and recourse to her own specially favoured patch of rough grass which had turned miserably yellow from daily libations, and she was ready to trot in for breakfast.

For the rest of the time, however, apart from her daily walks she was constantly with us in the house or car, living at a temperature better suited to humans than canines and, in retrospect, my own explanation for the skin troubles that began to plague her was that she was always slightly too hot. Dogs have no sweat glands and their skin is notably tough, which makes them slow to react to changes of temperature. I have seen my mother's labrador lie up against the bars of an electric fire until her fur was actually smoking. When she finally registered discomfort there were parallel ginger lines on her yellow coat where the hair was singed, but she appeared quite unbothered.

So was it overheating that made Jemima so itchy? Or could it have been connected to her status as quasi human, in effect our substitute child, and obliged continually to behave in a way that was contrary to her nature? A single dog in a household is treated very much as a human member of the family would be, whereas two dogs or more will form their own small pack, with a proper canine hierarchy, and behave in a way that is much more natural and therefore less stressful for them.

Here I am on shaky ground, scientifically speaking, but stress certainly exacerbates eczema, psoriasis and skin problems of the kind among susceptible humans, so might it not do the same for dogs?

When circumstances obliged a continually-itchy London-based beagle of our acquaintance, who lived a most undoglike life as the pet and sole companion of a highly-strung make-up artist, to board for a month in the country where he not only lived outdoors, but was able to bark and dig and run free in a big paddock with all the other dog-boarders, his skin improved out of all recognition. Instead of lying for hours at a time by his owner's computer or accompanying her to photo-shoots, he was able to revert to dog-dom, with spectacular results; but as soon as he returned to his old life his old problems recommenced.

At the time, where Jemima was concerned, I didn't attribute her skin troubles to the lack of canine company. Rather, because she constantly flapped her ears, we suspected mites and were prescribed bottle after bottle of very expensive emulsion – liquid gold, we called it – to squirt directly into the aural canal, a process none of us enjoyed. It did no discernible good.

'Must be an allergy,' said the vet, and prescribed special shampoos and lotions. Working these into her thick coat, lathering, rinsing and rubbing her dry was messy and time-consuming, and in true labrador fashion she would take the first opportunity to rid herself of the clinical smell by rolling in a cowpat, so would have to be hosed off anew.

That did no good either.

The condition got marginally better when we were in Scotland, out on the hill all day, but even then she would go into tormenting orgies of scratching at night, and since on holiday she had to share our bedroom none of us got much sleep.

As the vet's bills mounted and each remedy seemed more

useless than the last one, we reluctantly agreed to the nuclear option: steroids. These stopped the itching all right, but the side-effects – incontinence and a ravening appetite – were almost more dire than the condition itself.

By this time we were living on our own small farm, where there were countless temptations for a hungry dog. We hurdled off the muckheap and put bolts on every feedbin that might be lifted by a questing nose. Intense vigilance or a lead was necessary when crossing fields with grazing livestock to prevent her eating dung, while the chances of her finding and crunching up a myxy rabbit or the rotting carcase of a pheasant took much of the pleasure out of a stroll in the woods. Indoors I grew used to pushing all food well back from the edge of the kitchen table and work surfaces and, with a complicated arrangement of bars outside the windowsill where the cats' dishes were placed, Duff made their dining-area impregnable to attack by labrador.

Her most infamous feat occurred while she was being driven home from a shoot. Crowded into a small 4x4 vehicle were two men and their dogs, plus guns, game bags, cartridges, coats and, at the bottom of the heap, a brace of pheasants. Half a mile from home, a half-muffled cracking sound from the back alerted the passenger to trouble, and he was just in time to snatch the cock pheasant from Jemima's jaws – minus a leg.

Minutes later they drove into the farmyard, laughing and chatting, only to find as they sorted out their equipment that the hen pheasant had completely vanished. Feathers, beak, wings, legs – Jemima had gulped down the lot.

It was all a considerable nuisance but, on the plus side, her coat was glossy and thick again, and the flapping and scratching had stopped. It was a fine balance, but we reckoned the steroids were worth continuing – just.

Come August, our ram lambs went off to the local abattoir as usual, and were returned ten days later neatly packaged for the deep freeze, each with its bag of bones. After simmering some of these in the bottom oven, I skimmed the fat off the resulting stock, and put it in a plastic bucket – which it half-filled – meaning to bury it in the muckheap where Jemima could not get at it. At the time, I knew she was out for a walk so, when I took the opportunity to deviate into the tackroom as I passed, it seemed safe enough to put the bucket just momentarily on top of the old stone milkstand.

Big mistake. We had converted the milk-stand into a mounting block by building steps up one side, and when I emerged I saw with horror that Jemima had run back ahead of Duff, and had her head deep in the bucket, gulping down mutton fat in great mouthfuls as fast as she could.

If only, *if only* I had realised how dangerous this would prove. If only I had immediately pushed Epsom salts or bicarb, or even washing-soda down her throat to make her vomit up the fat!

As it was, I snatched the bucket away, thinking it might upset her digestion but nothing worse, and forgot the incident until, two evenings later, Jemima jumped off the sofa looking very hangdog, passed a horrible grey mess in the garden, then went unusually soberly to her bed in the kennel. By morning she was clearly uncomfortable and running a temperature, so I whisked her to the animal hospital.

We still didn't realise how serious it was, and after she had examined Jemima, I told the vet almost jokingly about the stolen mutton fat. To my surprise and alarm, she immediately proposed a scan, and said they would have to keep her at the hospital in case she needed an emergency operation.

Operation? I could hardly believe what I was hearing. After all, labradors are famous for their powers of digestion. Jemima's own mother had once eaten half a Stilton cheese without ill-effect, and on another occasion 5lbs of granulated sugar destined for marmalade-making. And what about that pheasant with its beak, feathers and claws?

'It looks like pancreatitis,' said the vet sombrely. 'There may be nothing we can do.'

Those are words you very seldom hear. I certainly hadn't. The veterinary profession is infinitely resourceful, infinitely inventive. There is always one more possible treatment, one more operation that will undoubtedly cost several thousand pounds and involve months of nursing, but will eventually put everything right. This sounded horribly like a death sentence, and so it proved.

'Her whole inside is blocked,' reported the vet a few hours later. 'Even if we operate there is no likelihood that she would recover.'

So Duff had to make the painful decision to put down the best dog he had ever owned and bring her home for burial, all because of a moment's inattention and my ignorance of canine First Aid.

People say that when a hitherto all-female college decides to admit men, a lot of rebuilding and reorganisation are necessary. New showers. Urinals. Locks on this and that. New rules. Playing fields have to be upgraded and sporting equipment bought to keep them happy, whereas girls can be added to a mens' college with minimal fuss or disruption.

In the same way when you add a dog to your household, you have to make all sorts of adjustments to your domestic arrangements. Where will it sleep? How can you protect the car-seats? What will it eat and drink out of? Who will care for it when you want to jet off to the sun? Then there is the question of fitting your life around the walks, the training, the regular lettings out of doors and enticing back in. Taking on a dog is, in short, a life-changing commitment, a major upheaval.

Cats, on the other hand, slip into a new home with scarcely a ripple to disturb the smooth surface of everyday life. It takes no more than a few hours to establish the essential taboos – no jumping on the kitchen table, no sitting on the nice warm PC keyboard – after that they carve out their own place in the household and fit it as neatly as conkers in their shell.

Acquiring a cat is so simple you can't help thinking: What's the catch? But in truth there is no catch. No need to study pedigrees or hip-scores. No need to splurge on polystyrene-filled cushions or dinky tunnels lined with fake sheepskin, because like as not the cats will scorn what you provide, preferring to make their own arrangements. As Roger McGough puts it: *Cats sleep anywhere/ Any table, any chair, / Top of cupboard, window ledge,/ In the middle, on the edge./ Anywhere, they don't care./ Cats sleep anywhere.*

When we first moved out of London, I didn't know any of this. I had never owned a cat and didn't want any pet capable of jumping on work-surfaces to lick the butter, killing birds and sicking up the remains in the linen cupboard, or any of the countless other felonies of which such an agile, athletic animal is capable. Although there was clear evidence of vermin about the barns and buildings, pest control was the province of the farm manager and his merry men, who set traps and put down poison as circumstance dictated.

So in the bleak midwinter when Nannie complained of mice and said we needed a cat to deal with them, I was less than keen. The truth was that I felt harassed and over-stretched, in no mood to add to my responsibilities, and was becoming ever more aware of the good sense behind Mr Jorrocks's famous dictum, *'Damn all presents wot eats.'* After four years at Bromsden Farm, in addition to the basic house-party of dogs and humans both adult and juvenile who required daily feeding, I had amassed too many four-legged dependents on too small a patch to sustain them year-round.

It was all very well to keep horses, hens and a couple of calves on three unthrifty acres in summer, when they could more or less feed themselves, but from November until April when there was no goodness in what grass there was, I was spending a large part of each day carting fodder from barn to field, filling haynets, mucking out.

Besides, there was a pheasant shoot on the estate and, having seen at first hand the mortality rate among his mother's cats when he was a boy and knowing that a catskin weskit is considered the peak of sartorial elegance by many gamekeepers, Duff warned against adding felines to the strength.

'Much better not. They don't last five minutes here.'

Undeterred, Nannie kept lobbying. Four-year-old Alice had recently come out in red spots all over her legs and on investigation a cosy mouse-nest had been uncovered in the blankets at the end of her bed.

'Flea-bites! That would never have happened if we'd had a cat,' said Nannie, 'and look at all those rabbits in the garden. You'll never grow a lettuce with them nibbling at the seedlings.'

The rabbits in the vegetable patch were indeed a pest. Reluctantly I gave in. 'But it will have to live outdoors. None of this lolling about on silken cushions,' I said, remembering my grandmother's pampered Siamese who had never caught a mouse in his life. 'We'll feed it outside, like a proper farmyard cat.'

'We'll see,' said Nannie, magnanimous in victory.

Round about my birthday, having taken advice locally, Duff visited to the nearest animal shelter and returned in triumph with rather a rarity –a striped ginger female whom the charity had not yet spayed. We installed her in a cosy corner of the toolshed, buttered her paws, and kept her confined there until she was settled. It was no surprise when, a couple of months later, she gave birth to four attractively-marked kittens. We decided to keep two.

Rainbow kittens for sale, I advertised, thinking other people would find them as beautiful as I did, but the first customers rudely dashed this hope.

'Nothing *rainbow* about them,' said the fussy, fidgety old husband with contempt, giving the kittens a cursory glance before hurrying his wife back into his car. 'Those are just ordinary tortoiseshells. No one's going to pay £5 for *them*. From the advert, I thought you'd got something special for sale.'

Luckily the next couple who rang were less demanding, and paid up happily enough for their common tortoiseshell kittens, but the first customer's words left a nasty taste in my mouth. One of the most disagreeable aspects of selling livestock is the way so many potential buyers feel obliged to denigrate and find fault with whatever they are offered, I suppose in the hope that the price will be reduced, though in my case the tactic has precisely the opposite effect and makes me decide instantly that whatever my animal's imperfections, I shall not allow it to fall into the hands of someone who despises it. Or even pretends to despise it.

I also feel that one should never *give* an animal away: people tend to value and look after what they have paid for much more than something they acquire for free.

So there we were with three outdoor cats on the strength, their feeding-station on the windowsill outside the kitchen, and their favourite lairs among the hay-bales in the barn. Though they would allow the occasional caress – when it suited them – they were fairly wild, but I enjoyed catching glimpses of them slinking about their daily affairs, concentrated, wary, and busy whether they were watching at a mousehole or grooming one another in the sun. Nor was there any doubt that their presence had an impact on the rabbits.

Yet all too soon, as Duff had warned, the Shoot's aversion to cats became overt. Walking back across the field one summer evening, I was horrified to see my ginger cat being chased homeward by the gamekeeper's son on his motorbike, zigzagging wildly from one side of the lane to the other until she fled into a barn with fur on end and tail curved into a terrified half-hoop.

I blocked the boy's path as he turned to ride away and gave him a piece of my mind, which did nothing to improve matters, and when about a week later the ginger cat disappeared entirely I had a fair idea we would never see her again. Nor did we, though as usual in the country by roundabout ways word of what had become of her finally reached us. In the summer gloaming she had been seen in the hedgerow near the pheasants' release pen, mistaken for a fox and shot dead. The gamekeeper was sorry, but he had to look after his birds. Etc etc.

Useless to rage that if he couldn't distinguish between a cat and a fox he shouldn't have fired at all. Apart from shutting them indoors, there is really no way of stopping cats hunting, but the untimely death of poor Ginge made me realise that if we didn't want the kittens to suffer the same fate we would have to alter their lifestyle asap.

They were now seven months old, lean and rangy, both female, and difficult to tell apart from a distance, though close up you could see that one's fluffy coat made her look fatter than her smooth sister.

'You ought to get those spayed unless you want to be overrun with cats,' remarked my sister-in-law one day, watching them as they sat on a wall in provocative attitudes, challenging her Jack Russells to have a go.

'Oh, surely not yet! They're only kittens.'

'Tomcats don't hang about, you know.'

So I made an appointment with the vet and, at the cost of some spectacular scratches, managed to catch and cram them into a travel-box. Throughout the five-mile journey they yowled at earsplitting volume and scrabbled against the weld-mesh until their paws and faces were pouring blood. Heads jerked round as I entered the surgery, and disapproving eyes followed as I clumped across the shiny lino from reception desk to consulting room clutching the dripping cage at arm's length, with a mop-wielding nurse close behind.

'Been in the wars, have we?' said the vet, surveying his patients warily and filling a syringe. 'All right, set them down; we'll take over now.'

I left, feeling a heel to abandon them in this strange, chemical-smelling place, and worse when I picked them up some hours later, still groggy from the anaesthetic, eyes glazed, paws bandaged and taped, and each with one shaven flank and a neatly stitched wound. Sure enough, they had both been pregnant.

'Keep them quiet for a couple of days and they'll be right as rain,' said the cheerful receptionist. 'You can take the stitches out yourself in about a week or, if you can't manage, bring them back and we'll do it.'

Knowing that wild horses weren't going to get them back into that travelling-box, I co-opted a steely-nerved friend to help with do-it-yourself stitch-removal and resolved on an all-out effort to tame the little cats before the week was over. As it turned out, I needn't have worried. The operation had had a miraculously calming effect on them, and when they regained full consciousness and explored the house, the cats seemed charmed with their new surroundings. Fat and Thin, as we continued to call them since changing an animal's name is said to be unlucky and no one wanted to tempt Fate, made no effort to resume their wild life in the barns. They took possession of the chairs on either side of the fire, and entered into their role as domestic pets with enthusiasm.

'I knew you'd come round in the end,' said Nannie complacently.

Though I wasn't going to admit it, I had more than come round: after a few days of their company I was a complete convert, bowled over by feline charm. They were simply no trouble at all. Not only did they quietly arrange their lives around ours and need no instruction or formal exercise, but from the first they were perfectly house-trained, scrupulously scraping a small hole in which to deposit faeces, then raking the soil back with great care, shaking their paws clear of earth with a few disdainful flicks.

Nor was there any problem with the dogs, who appeared to realise they were now a permanent part of the household and must not be harassed. The mouse problem vanished as quickly as it had arisen; I wondered why I had tried to bar them from the house in the first place.

Far from needing doors opened and shut for them, the cats came and went as they pleased through a self-closing flap, whose function they mastered overnight, its distinctive click-*clack* announcing to anyone in the kitchen that the hunters had returned and were in need of grub. That was really the only demand they made on me, although like all cats they had the irritating habit of leaving a few bites in the bottom of the bowl as insurance against night starvation. Since this was a magnet for flies, I would throw it away, and grew to admire the ingenuity with which they would convey to me that their dishes needed a refill. Whatever time of day they felt hungry (depending, I suppose, on whether or not a hunt had been successful) they would seek me out in garden, study, or stable, and become very charming, parading along fences or sprawling among my papers until I was forced to acknowledge their presence.

Next they would approach and solicit stroking, curling round my legs and, if I still didn't get the message, sit staring unblinkingly and utter single mews precisely pitched at the timbre most annoying to the human ear, spacing the sounds until they were as impossible to ignore as a dripping tap.

The moment I put down whatever I was doing and turned to attend to the distraction, they would trot rapidly towards the kitchen, look round to see I was following and, if I happened to deviate from the direct line, return to the mewing and leg-winding until they again got me moving in the right direction. Considering our relative sizes, it was a highly skilled piece of manipulation – mind over matter, one might say – and I very soon discovered it was less trouble to give up at once and submit to their wishes.

For fourteen years they kept us company, becoming tamer as time passed, but always accepting petting with a slight air of condescension and moving away if any human showed signs of wanting to pick them up. They preferred to keep their paws on the ground. When they died, which they did within a few months of one another, it was with minimal fuss. Riveted to *Dr Who*, I saw from the tail of my eye the survivor, Thin, get up from her favourite place on the nursery hearth-rug and slip quietly behind an armchair; minutes later, as the credits rolled, I looked to see where she had gone and found her stretched out, dead.

From then on, cats have always been part of our household, two at a time for choice, generally brother and sister (neutered for everyone's peace of mind) and though no one could claim they haven't a few uncultured habits, by and large I would rate them the most civilised of all household pets.

Some have been mighty hunters: Jasper – who began life named Jasmine until a vet pointed out the obvious – used to tug whole pheasants and pigeons through the cat-flap and pluck them on the dining-room carpet. We never ascertained whether he caught them roosting or picked them up after a shoot, but since they were perfectly fresh and he only ate the heads, Duff would remove them when he had had his fill and lay sprawled and satisfied, skin the untouched legs and breasts and I would cook them for our own supper. It seemed a fair division of spoils.

Jasper also enjoyed an evening walk with or without the dogs, sauntering along waving his tail a few paces behind when I went round checking the livestock, and should he encounter a young lamb that had strayed too far from its mother, he would go into an extravagantly playful routine: rolling on his back, tossing a pebble in his paws, lying supine until the fascinated lamb approached, stretching out an exploratory nose, then moving away a few feet to entice it still farther away from maternal surveillance. Clearly it was an act as carefully choreographed as that of the stoat which stands on its hind legs and weaves from side to side to hypnotise a rabbit, though just what Jasper thought he would do when he had the lamb at his mercy is impossible to say. Did he mean to spring on its back like a mountain lion, wrench its head back and with one bite sever the spinal cord?

I'll never know, because the scenario always ended the same way. A shout from me, a bleat from the lamb, and up would bustle the ewe to teach the marauder a lesson.

'Spoilsport,' Jasper's look would say as we resumed our evening walk.

Of all our cats he was the most self-sufficient, and if push came to shove could very well have fed himself without human assistance. By nature he was autocratic and possessive. When he wanted something, he wanted it *now* – at once, no messing – and we were fortunate that it was only in extreme old age that he hit on the surefire way to secure immediate attention.

I was chatting on the telephone one evening, leaning against the fridge and fending off Jasper's demand that I should open it and take out the raw liver he so loved with my usual mantra: 'Hang on a tick, can't you see I'm busy?' when he stopped winding round my legs, backed up and deliberately squirted urine almost as high as my waist.

When this occurs, on no account should you jump and scream because this will reinforce his behaviour, advised the *Daily Telegraph's* animal problem guru. *Nor should you scold him since that means he has succeeded in securing your attention. The best strategy is to leave the room quietly...*

Easier said than done. Mercifully he perpetrated the outrage only three or four times, but this was because I was extremely wary of his food-soliciting overtures from then on, and on the occasions when he did take me by surprise, I not only jumped and screamed but also cursed and kicked out at him. I defy anyone to behave otherwise.

He was a cat of great character, yet in some ways it was a relief when the Grim Reaper intervened, and Jasper joined his sister and several of their predecessors under the Cryptomeria within sight of the kitchen door.

One summer day, nine-year-old Alice came home fizzing with excitement about the new project her class was doing on Bees and Honey, and bombarded us with amazing facts and statistics. Did we know that bees had to fly the equivalent of *three times round the world* to produce a single pound of honey? Or that the hexagonal cells in a honeycomb were *geometrically perfect,* incapable of improvement? Or that when a worker bee found a source of nectar, she told her mates exactly where it was by *dancing to the points of the compass?*

No, we said, and No again, and presently, infected by her enthusiasm and the tempting prospect of a hundredweight of honey from a single colony – 'in a good year,' Alice added cautiously – we agreed that it was high time we added a hive, a queen, and a nucleus of gentle, good-tempered bees to the strength.

For complete beginners, the obvious first step was to seek advice from local experts, and no one could have been more ready to dispense it than the longstanding secretary of the nearest association of apiarists. Bee-keepers are enthusiasts, and the faintest show of interest from an outsider fires them with messianic zeal to spread the word about the powers and wonders of their charges. I found that the real difficulty was to get a word in edgeways.

Amid the flood of verbiage, two contradictory messages came through loud and clear. The first was that everyone should keep bees. It was good for the natural world, beneficial for humans, and it couldn't be easier. Put bees in a hive, substitute sugar syrup for the honey you removed, and bob's your uncle, nature would do the rest.

The second message I picked up was starkly different. To maintain the health of a colony demanded constant vigilance, skill, and experience, and unless you timed everything right, you would be lucky to harvest any honey at all.

So which was I to believe?

Though I found this difficult to grasp at the time, both messages were perfectly true. For long periods of the bee-keeping year, the complex life of the hive carries on happily without human interference, and nothing could be easier than looking after the inhabitants. But should the weather be unseasonable – warm in February, for example, so the bees emerge from hibernation and find no nectar, or cold in July, which obliges the colony to consume winter stores when they should be built up – the bees may starve unless immediately supplied with sugar syrup to make up the nectar deficiency.

Since the hive should only be opened when the temperature is 70 degrees or over, a chilly, wet summer is very bad news, and instead of harvesting the fabled hundredweight of honey, the tyro bee-keeper is likely to find himself out of pocket after bulk-buying sugar for his poor hungry workers.

From the initial wave of our friendly apiarist's advice, however, we disentangled two basic recommendations: the box-like 'National' hive would be the easiest for us to start on; and the most suitable nucleus of bees for beginners to handle would be the laid-back, yellow Italian variety bred by Brother Ambrose at Buckfast Abbey, in Devon.

The queen, however, we ordered from America.

Following instructions, we assembled the hive in a sunny

corner of the garden, sheltered from the east wind by a high
hedge, well away from the house and stables. The basic kit
contained a deep lower compartment, known as a double brood
chamber, with a shallower upper storey in which the honey would
be stored. The flat, waxy, foundation frames with projecting
wooden lugs, which the workers would draw out into proper
honeycombs, smelled delicious, and slotted neatly into racks,
though as living, eating, and breeding quarters they looked to
me extremely claustrophobic. The spacing of the racks is critical,
we were told, and must be no more or less than a quarter of an
inch, since any wider passage would be used by the bees to build
up extra comb, while a narrower gap would be sealed with the
waxy yellow secretion known as propolis.

This two-tiered dwelling was topped with a plywood
'crown board,' with a zinc-covered lid, tight-fitting to prevent
it being blown off, and doubly protected against this danger by
placing a heavy stone on top. The brood chamber had a narrow
slot of entrance, too low to admit a mouse, and a projecting lip
of 'flight board' on which the bees could take off and land. This
was sloped downward to prevent water running into the hive,
and the whole edifice placed on a plinth of concrete blocks, to
minimise the need for grass-mowing.

We were warned that bees disliked any kind of disturbance.
The smell of horses was anathema to them, and so were expensive
scent, brightly-coloured clothes, loud voices, and the noise of
mowing machines, while thundery weather was guaranteed to
make them stroppy. All in all, they were pretty sensitive souls,
and their sole form of protest was to attack and sting the source
of annoyance, even though they died as a result.

Thoughtfully, we scanned the bee-keeping catalogues
and ordered protective all-in-one suits, broad-brimmed hats
with integral veils, and long-gauntleted kid-gloves to protect us
from our new charges. That first taste of home-produced honey
looked like being an expensive one.

There were other, equally essential tools to buy. An extractor, like a spindryer with a tap at the base, in which to whirl the loaded combs and release the golden flow of honey by centrifugal force. A ripener, in which to store the thin honey until it reached the right stage of viscosity for bottling. Then we needed a smoker, a sort of hand-bellows attached to a canister with a bent nozzle, in which to burn corrugated paper in order to trick the bees into thinking there was a forest fire. Their instinct would then be to tank up with as much nectar as they could ingest, and this in turn made them feel sleepy and calm. The theory was that you could then handle them safely, remove frames of honey or scrape encrusted propolis from the crown board, without fear of attack. Another essential was the 'hive tool' – a long metal scraper which doubled up as a screwdriver – and the slotted zinc sheet known as a 'queen excluder,' because it stopped the queen laying brood among the honey cells in the hive's top layer.

The next excitement was the arrival of our new colony's nucleus. Their travelling-box was prominently marked *LIVE BEES, THIS WAY UP,* and emitted a low hum. The carrier placed it on the kitchen table very gently, and with equal care Duff carried it out to the sheltered corner where the hive awaited its inhabitants, and for a time we all stood round admiring it, screwing up our nerve to open the hinged lid. It was a warm, still, summer morning, perfect for bee-handling, but for some reason we found it difficult to get started.

'Better tog up,' I suggested nervously.

I, at least, felt bolder when we were both dressed from head to toe in thick snowy suits, elasticated at wrists and ankle, gumboots, long gloves and veiled hats. With some difficulty, Duff lit the smoker and when it was going satisfactorily he unscrewed the box's fastening, puffed some smoke into the gauze cover of the lid, and gently eased it open.

The hum grew momentarily louder, then settled back to

its low key. One by one, he lifted out the four frames smothered in yellow-banded golden bees, and hung them in the prepared broodchamber. Inevitably some fell back into the travelling-box during this operation, so he tipped it upside down over the newly installed frames and gave it a sharp tap to dislodge any lingerers before replacing the lid.

By this time, the note of the buzzing was steadily rising and some militant-looking bees were circling both us and the hive. Despite full protection, I expected at any moment to feel a stab of pain, but the smoke had worked its magic and we completed the operation without being stung.

A few days later, the queen arrived by airmail, correctly stamped and labelled. Her ingenious little cage was carved from a solid block of wood a few inches in length, with a gauze-covered airhole, and each end sealed with a plug of hard sugar candy. These were in order to prevent the workers attacking and killing her as an intruder: by the time they had nibbled through the candy, they would be accustomed to her smell and treat her as one of themselves.

Or nearly. Even I could see that she didn't look like a worker bee. She was longer, slimmer; her wings were folded flatter, and the enlarged abdomen which contained uncounted thousands of eggs stretched from behind her second pair of legs to the tip of her tail. With growing confidence I dressed again from head to foot in protective gear, lit the smoker, and opened the hive to install her among her subjects.

We had been warned that the colony would need support during its first season, and fed it religiously throughout the summer with the prescribed syrup – 2lbs sugar dissolved in 1 pint of water. Sure enough, when we opened the 'super,' or top storey of the hive in late July, only a few of the combs were full and capped, so we limited ourselves to taking a single one, just to prove that the whole enterprise was worthwhile.

The following season, however, we had a bumper crop:

thirty-odd pounds of the most delicate pale, fragrant honey imaginable, tasting of flowers and trees, clover and lime-blossom, which filled every jampot in the house. Duff commissioned an artist to design an elegant label, and I, at least, began to consider myself quite an old hand at the bee-keeping game.

At this stage of the saga, I was the principal apiarist, since Alice's interest had waned as soon as the class's project was finished. I read bee-keeping magazines, joined the local association and attended its lectures. As time went on and nothing serious went wrong, my initial fear was replaced by a somewhat gung-ho confidence which soon descended into carelessness.

One sultry afternoon in July, I went to carry out a routine inspection, dressed as usual in hat and veil, white suit and gloves, and carrying the smoker, but quite forgot that I was wearing sandals rather than rubber boots. All was quiet as I approached the hive from behind, removed the lid, and placed the whole top storey – the 'super' – on top of it in order to peer into the brood chamber itself.

The normal buzzing went up a couple of notes, and bees poured out of the open top to see what I was up to, but within the veil I felt perfectly secure and carried on inspecting the combs until a sudden sharp pain in the instep alerted me to danger. Glancing down, I saw with horror that I seemed to be wearing thick fur boots. Moving boots. With unerring precision, the bees had recognised my one vulnerable point, and settled there in their thousands in order to sting the intruder to death.

I banged the lid back on the hive any old how, and ran for the house, kicking frantically to dislodge my attackers.

'Don't bring them into the house!' called Nannie, yanking the children into the nursery and slamming the door. A moment later her hand came out again, holding a can of aerosol wasp-killer, and this I sprayed lavishly at my feet and legs, until all the poor brave bees lay in drifts on the kitchen floor. Already the elasticated hems of my suit were cutting into my legs as they swelled. By the time I had stripped it off both feet and legs were swollen like bolsters, red and shiny and speckled with the little black lances of bee-stings, my whole body felt on fire and my heart was hammering as if it would choke me.

Too late I remembered my father's face and neck turning a terrifying purple as he flung himself fully dressed into a cold bath after a mere wasp-sting, and my sister Miranda's near-panic when she forded a Spanish river on a horse and found ranks of hives lined up on the farther bank. Plainly I had inherited the same allergy.

'Don't let this happen again,' said the doctor, pumping in drugs. 'Anaphylactic shock can kill you once you've become sensitised to whatever causes it.'

So bang went my career as a hands-on apiarist, and Duff bravely took charge of the bees from that day on, while I watched from a safe distance and dished out advice. He, too, was stung from time to time but fortunately reacted much less violently. He also took the sensible step of recruiting help in the form of Bill, a neighbour's gardener, a thin, saturnine, former Navy cook whose family had kept bees for generations. Cursing steadily, he would handle swarms with only a wisp of veiling for protection.

'Think I 'ad injection then,' he would say, slapping unconcernedly. His sangfroid made the whole business of being stung seem much less of a drama.

A perennial problem for the bee-keeper is swarming. This strange instinct kicks in when the colony feels itself overcrowded, or is upset by too much handling, or even because they fancy a new source of nectar and reckon that their existing territory is played out. Whatever the particular reason, the result is the same. The colony rears a new queen, who briskly kills off the occupants of all other queen cells, and the old one takes flight, accompanied by a large proportion of her subjects.

Unless you see this happen, and track the swarm to the

bush, fence-post, branch, or building on which it settles while sending out scouts to find a new permanent home, your colony is weakened by the loss of so many workers and foragers, and its honey harvest correspondingly reduced. Since this may happen several times during the summer, bee-keepers are always on the alert for signs of new queen cells in the brood chamber, and do their best to destroy them before they hatch.

Capturing a swarm is an exciting business, demanding a cool head and steady hand. First you notice unusual activity round the hive, round which bees start to circle instead of flying directly to or from the flight board. As their numbers build up, normal buzzing becomes a muted roar until suddenly they form a dense cloud and, with unstoppable momentum, zoom away into the far blue yonder.

Providing the bee-keeper actually sees them go, he can do his best to induce them to land by spraying them with water from a handy hose, or pursue them with a water-bucket and powerful syringe. Bill, our fearless guru, believed in the old-fashioned method of banging gongs and clashing saucepans, and it was a fine sight to see him chasing the swarm thus armed, leaping fences and crashing through brambles until his quarry settled into a gently-pulsing, heart-shaped lump with the queen closely protected at its centre.

Where it settled dictated the next stage of the operation. So long as the swarm hung from a branch, bush, or anything else that could be shaken, it was a relatively simple matter to place a log-basket or a cardboard box underneath and, with a sudden sharp tug, dislodge the whole slippery mass of bees into it. A few outliers might miss the receptacle, but so long as the queen was in it, the bulk of the swarm would remain with her.

Less easy to manage was a swarm that attached itself to an upright post, window frame, or the trunk of a tree. Capturing this might involve delicately sweeping the bees into the box or skep with a soft brush; or, if their landing place had been a thick bush, puffing smoke beneath it to induce the bees to crawl upwards into the inverted box.

Every case demanded a different approach, which lent the whole operation a thrillingly ad hoc flavour, and each captured swarm was a triumph of improvisation, nerve and determination. Once the bees were safely shut in their temporary prison, you had to wait until evening and then, while the light was still good enough, tip them on to a board propped against the hive, and watch for the queen as her workers escorted her home.

So tightly did they cluster round her, however, that sometimes the only clue to her presence was a sort of rolling wave in the hundreds of insects crawling up the improvised ramp. Bill used to pick up handfuls, wherever the population was thickest, and spread them out, to see where they would try to cluster again, because that was where he would find the queen. Once spotted, she was quickly killed, whereupon the rest of the bees would calmly make their way into the hive again, to work for the young queen who had succeeded her.

One very hot morning, while Duff was lecturing to members of the local Deer Society, who had formed a semicircle under our walnut tree, he noticed that the attention of the back rows seemed to be wandering. Afraid that he was boring them, he speeded up his discourse, skipping several interesting points, but still his audience seemed uneasy, turning their heads and looking nervously skywards.

Then as the sky darkened and a low roar, as of an incoming plane, sent his audience scuttling towards the house, he saw a thick cloud of bees leave the hive and whirl around the walnut tree in ever-decreasing circles until it finally coalesced in a huge bulb-shaped lump on the branch from which Alice's trapeze was suspended.

However much he tried to persuade them that the bees were now no threat to them, there was no way of persuading the audience back to their seats, so the lecture was concluded indoors.

Less than three feet or more than three miles is the rule of thumb for shifting hives, so our move from Oxfordshire to our new home in Gloucestershire presented the bees with no problems of orientation. Move the hive a mere five feet, however, and you are in trouble because the foragers will return and sit pathetically on the ground where the hive used to be until they die of cold and hunger.

Thus when we were offered another hive complete with its colony by a friend who lived just a mile away, Duff had the ridiculous task of driving the whole caboodle to a garden five miles away, leaving it a couple of weeks until the bees were nicely settled and had forgotten their original home, and then scooping it up again at dusk and driving it back to our own orchard. During the second part of this operation, the lid became dislodged, allowing a number of bees to escape. Hastily switching on the blower of the air-conditioning to pin them to the back window, he hurtled along the narrow lanes and reached home unscathed, but it was an unnerving experience.

In the new orchard, within easy range of the house, the two hives flourished and their occupants did a great job of fertilising the fruit trees. Unfortunately, however, it was near a field gate, and when I went to bring in my horse one evening I found him in a stupor, his pretty Araby face and neat muzzle so swollen that he looked like a cow, while his whole body was quilted with lumps.

That cost £60-worth of antihistamine jabs, plus a week's box rest before I dared put a saddle on him and girth it up, and this latest incident impelled us to move the hives away to our farthest boundary.

Out of sight, out of mind. It became progressively more difficult to remember to visit the hives frequently, taking all the necessary equipment in a wheelbarrow, and gaps between inspections became longer. There is a kernel of truth in the Old Wives' Dictum that you must tell your bees about any significant event in the family: Births, Deaths, Marriages and so on, because if you fail to keep them informed, they will leave you. As we grew gradually out of touch with our own colony, honey yields declined. We must have failed to see swarms leaving home, or to feed the bees at the right moment and, one year, after an unseasonably warm early spring, we discovered that one colony had perished and the other looked sickly, with only half a dozen frames still in use.

Was it disease? Bees are prone to a number of killer ailments such as foul brood, when the combs turn black and soggy, or dysentery, which leaves the hive smeared with smelly brown fluid. Another major cause of ill-health is parasite attack, the most common being the varroa mite, and *nosema apis,* which attacks the wall of the stomach. To combat these pests, you are advised to hang a strip of insecticide-impregnated wax inside the hive, but so disgusting does it smell that it takes away all the pleasure from eating honey that has been made in close proximity to the chemical. So we left it out, and though the colony struggled on for another season, there was no surplus honey, nor did lavish winter feeding give it a noticeable boost.

The final nail in the coffin of our honey-production was hammered home when our farming neighbours planted an extensive acreage of oilseed rape well within the foraging area of our worker bees.

The sickly-sweet scent of the bright yellow flowers drew them like a magnet and the colony went into overdrive, filling frame after frame with a thick, gluey, white honey which set so hard, so quickly, that it was impossible to extract. Normally, after slicing off the wax capping, a few minutes of rapid spinning in the extractor would empty the frames and leave liquid honey to run out through the tap at the bottom. With rape honey, the frames came out of the extractor just as heavy as they had gone in. It was unshiftable, and our only means of harvesting it was to cut out chunks of comb, which wrecked the frames and was difficult to store.

To add insult to injury, the honey itself had the same over-sweet sickliness as the rape flowers. It tasted just like low-grade commercial honey – the kind they give racehorses – which is probably mass-produced from oilseed rape rather than blossom.

We returned the mutilated frames for the bees to clean up, as usual, and agreed that while rape continues to attract sky-high subsidies, keeping bees in this neck of the woods is just not worth the effort involved.

Nevertheless, as I am well aware, this is entirely the wrong attitude. Far from scrapping our beehives, we should be increasing them, encouraging the formation of new colonies and doing everything in our power to counter the alarming decline in England's bee population. And not only England's. All over the world colony collapse is a major headache for farmers and fruit-growers, yet it has generated few headlines and pitifully little research into its cause or causes.

Without much hard evidence, the blame has been variously laid on pesticides, or monoculture, or parasites, but no scientific body seems to have seriously addressed the possibility that today's bombardment of the world's airwaves by signals from wireless networks, mobile phones, and computers have disrupted the bees' delicate orientation system. When they leave the hive in search of pollen and nectar, they cannot find their way back, so starve to death.

Even if this is the case, it is hard to imagine modern man giving up his love of instant communication for the sake of saving bees; but whenever I see teenagers strolling the streets with heads crooked to the side, prattling mindlessly into their fancy mobiles, I wonder how they will cope in twenty years' time in a honey-less, fruit-less, veg-less world where Nature's pollinators have been driven to the brink of extinction through the over-use of Facebook and Twitter.

CHAPTER THREE

Tales from the Tackroom

NO ONE COULD claim that horses are an economic asset to a smallholding. Even after the initial expense of buying them, to keep them shod, fed, groomed, equipped and healthy weighs heavily on the balance sheet, and makes the yachtsman's definition of his sport as standing under a shower ripping up £50 notes look downright penny-pinching.

But who can put a price on pleasure? How can you measure beauty? What other animal can transform you from plodding earthling to son of the wind merely by allowing you upon its back? Such strength and speed, such versatility and goodwill! For never-diminishing enjoyment, interest and fun, the opportunity to keep a horse – or preferably two – is the greatest joy of living in the countryside.

The well-worn cliché that there's nothing so good for the inside of a man as the outside of a horse is perfectly true though I would add that, given the disparity between the amount of time spent actually in the saddle and the amount spent looking after your horse, you must enjoy what comes with it just as much as riding itself. Ah, the joys of mucking out, clipping, and grooming! Oh, the pleasures of washing rugs and soaping saddles! I'm not joking: I love it all, and that is why very soon after moving out of London we set about building a stable and filling it.

As well as costing a lot in money terms, there's no denying that horses require considerable investment in time and effort. Even if you've got a field, water-trough and shelter, you can't just turn out a pony and hope it will look after itself. So many things can go wrong that the owner's ever-vigilant eye is essential. Though I like to think I keep my horses as economically as possible – own labour, own pasture – and have never been tempted by competition with its stern disciplines and astronomical costs, I still can't face totting up with any degree of honesty exactly what I spend annually on matters connected with the stable – and that is before time is added to the account.

The briefest inspection of the tack-room gives the game away. There, ranged on hooks, on shelves or in drawers, are so many relics and reminders of different horses we have owned, top-quality saddlery and clothing that were useful in their day and are still too good to throw out, but which, realistically, no one is likely to use again. In total they represent a really horrifying expenditure.

Very few horses are perfect rides, some go too fast and some too slow, some carry their heads in the air or have a disconcerting tendency to buck, rear, nap, or indulge in some other form of equine wickedness which I, like most other owners, have always sought to counter by buying *just one more* set of boots, or a different bit, or a cat's cradle of complicated straps (known collectively in family-speak as 'hooping farthingales') which, I am convinced, will banish the problem. Of course they hardly ever do, but hope springs eternal and the alluring smell of new leather, the enticing heaps of brightly coloured ropes and rugs, saddles and bandages, have too often proved irresistible.

There, for instance, among once-necessary, now redundant treasures is the extra-long folded-leather girth I had made to measure when my own little thoroughbred mare, Dino, who had never been quite up to my weight, died suddenly, and my uncle very handsomely softened the blow by offering me a big bay ex-'chaser on permanent loan as a substitute. Who could turn down such a proposal?

Preciway was of distinguished lineage, his sire being Preciptic, and his relations included many stars both of flat-racing and over the sticks, notably those whose names began Pre – Premonition, Precipice Wood, Precipitation and so on – but his own career had been patchy. He never shone very brightly on the racecourse, though he had tried most things, first on the Flat in France, then over hurdles and eventually moving on to steeplechasing in England, where the height of his achievement was to win – against all expectations – a three-mile race at Newbury at Tote odds of 92–1.

'That's nearly £500, darling,' gloated my grandmother in triumph. She had, with unswerving loyalty through many disappointments, asked my mother to put yet another fiver to win on Preciway. At last, she thought, her son's horse had come up trumps.

But alas, Mummy had taken advice from his wily old trainer, who told her the horse was only half fit and unlikely to get the trip. She had therefore, with the kind intention of saving her mother's fiver, failed to place the bet. Gritting her teeth, she felt honour bound to pay Granny with her own money, which slightly prejudiced her against Preciway. He never won again, finally breaking down and being pronounced unfit for further racing. That was when he was offered to me.

'Breaking down' is a blanket term that covers differing degrees of injury, and many a horse recovers enough for less serious work than galloping and jumping at full speed. Six weeks later, when Preciway was said to be sound again, I went to look at him.

High on the Wiltshire Downs, alone in a bare, stony paddock on a bleak day in early Spring stood this gaunt, dejected animal with prominent hipbones and sharp high withers, hunched against the wind, looking like a giant toast-rack coated in mud, with long coarse 'cat-hairs' sticking out of his otherwise clipped coat. No company, no rug, no forage except some hay scattered at random, plus what he could grub from the muddy ground. His head was hanging low and looked much too big for his thin neck, but he raised it, cocking his ears and whinnying in a hopeful way, then stood looking after me as I went back down the hill.

'The poorer he gets, the quicker he'll mend,' growled his trainer when I tentatively questioned this treatment. He was probably right, but to anyone not in the racing game it seemed pretty rough on a horse to be rugged and cossetted and fed like a prince until he was injured, then turned out to fend for himself on a bleak, windy hillside. At once I made arrangements to collect him.

The arrival of Preciway at Bromsden had echoes of Gulliver's incursion into Lilliput. At 16.3 h h, long and rangy in build, he was much the biggest horse we had ever stabled in the wooden shed which Duff and Bert, a local handyman, had built at the bottom of the garden, and inevitably most of my existing tack was too small for him. As well as the folded leather girth, I had to buy a new bridle and headcollar, new rugs and an enormous striped wool blanket, and raise the height of rings and brackets for buckets – this last bit of adjustment less for the horse's benefit but to stop his companion donkey from guzzling half his rations.

Introducing him to Donk was hair-raising. We did it the approved way, letting Preciway settle into his new field for a few hours before bringing the donkey to the gate, whereupon the big horse trotted up with bulging eyes and ears braced forward, gave a trumpet blast down his nostrils and bolted for the fence at the far end – no great distance in so small a paddock – and it looked to me touch and go whether he would fly it and crash into the trees, wrecking his leg all over again.

In the last two yards he skidded to a halt, whirled round, galloped back for another horrified look at the furry stranger,

and hightailed off again round the field, dodging trees and drain covers while Donk, who was a friendly chap, compounded the problem by lifting his head and releasing a heartrending bray.

'Take him away,' I said urgently, handing Duff the lead-rope, and myself dashed to get halter and bucket in the hope of catching Precy and calming him down. Donk was reluctant to leave and had to be dragged away, braying in protest, and it was several fraught minutes before I managed to get a headcollar on the horse and lead him, sweating and shaking, into the stable.

It was a problem we hadn't expected. The two simply had to get used to one another if they were to share a field since I had nowhere else to put either of them. I couldn't understand it. All the other horses we had kept had loved Donk and indulged him even to the degree of letting him share buckets and haynets.

Over the next few days we niggled them closer by degrees, keeping both under restraint as we groomed them on opposite sides of the fence, progressed to leading them down the lane side by side, letting them sniff over the stable door and finally turning Precy into the field again while Donk yearned over the gate of the tiny yard. By evening they were fraternising warily, and the following day – hard-heartedly docking them both of breakfast – I risked turning them out together again. After an anxious half hour while Donk made overtures and Precy warily retreated, they settled down to graze on opposite sides of the paddock and that was the end of the trouble. A month later they were inseparable, sharing everything including the stable, and when my uncle came to see how his horse had adapted to his new life, he nicknamed them 'Les Deux Gugusses,' after the French clowns.

Apart from his fear of donkeys, Preciway was the most laid-back character imaginable. 'Seen that, been there, done that,' was his motto, and his wide experience of travelling, training, schooling, and racing crowds made him pretty well bomb-proof in situations other horses found stressful. The only time I remember him getting over-excited was when we passed a game of football: I suppose the keyed-up men in bright shirts reminded him of jockeys coming into the paddock.

He took to hunting with enthusiasm and I found it a great thrill to ride this perfectly biddable Rolls Royce of a horse, who could easily out-gallop and out-jump the rest of the Field, but was equally prepared to stand calmly when there was nothing going on. He even acted as lead-master when I took Alice to her first Pony Club meet on her Dartmoor pony, Nutty, who had to take about four strides to every one of Preciway's, but in the bath that night I found Alice's thigh black and blue with bruises from banging against my stirrup and we decided to leave her entirely to the care of Nutty in future.

Plenty of reminders of Nutty – full name Gingernut – still lurk about the tackroom. Her tiny rugs, her elastic-sided safety stirrups, and most treasured of all, her brass-mounted driving-harness, complete with breast-collar sporting a bell engraved *Victoria*, and probably dating from the last years of the old Queen's reign. I bought it for a tenner from the retiring proprietor of a seaside donkey-rides outfit, and for a time Donk wore it to pull a small light exercise cart. He was, like all donkeys, only moderately receptive to instructions, and we never dared to take him on the roads since his cavalier attitude to traffic might have ended in disaster.

With Nutty between the shafts it was a different matter. She fairly rattled along, steady as a rock whatever the traffic. When Alice was nine she used to drive her the three miles from Bromsden to Nettlebed to buy what we called Indelicatessen – ie basic stores – from the village shop, because I knew of no rule or by-law that a child has to attain a particular age before driving a pony and cart on the King's Highway. I always supposed that she took the lane through the woods, and only drove on the road within the village's speed limit zone, so was somewhat taken aback when accosted in the supermarket by a bossy neighbour.

'I must say I'm surprised you let your little girl drive that pony up the A423,' she said accusingly. 'There's such a lot of traffic. I'd never be brave enough to risk it.'

Whoops! Alice on the very straight, very fast, main road through the woods? I shot home to scold her, but she took the wind out of my sails by pointing out that I had never specified which way she was to go, and the lane was so rough and potholed that they couldn't go faster than a walk. Besides, the main road was safer. Drivers could see the cart from a long way away, and always slowed down to give her a wide berth and a friendly wave. All true enough, but even so Mrs Bosspot's words had spooked me, and I decreed that for the moment, at least, the shopping trips must stop.

Driving was only Nutty's second string, however. First and foremost she was a gymkhana pony, winning the serried rows of multi-coloured rosettes in the tackroom that now fascinate my grandchildren.

'You mean *Mummy* won all those?'

Sack Race. Gretna Green. Bending. Musical Chairs. Each has its date and provenance inscribed on the back and each represents a triumph for Nutty and a nail-biting few minutes for me. Though only 10.3 hands high and so broad in the back that no saddle but an inherently unstable pad anchored with a crupper would fit her, Nutty was nevertheless quick on her feet, and she and Alice shared a strong competitive instinct. Where other ponies galloped, she trotted like a metronome, ever-ready to wheel round, pull up, or accurately perform any other manoeuvre the race called for.

Thus in bending, while other children charged up the line and struggled to wrench their ponies round the end pole, Nutty would change direction without breaking stride and be weaving calmly towards the finish. Balancing potatoes on poles is a doddle if the pony stands still; almost impossible if it won't, and Musical Chairs, in which they specialised, involves so much vaulting on and off that a very small pony is a distinct plus.

Jumping was not her forte, but success in gymkhanas continued for years. As Alice grew tall and long-legged and Nutty remained the same size, I used to hear muttering at the ringside. 'Look at that child! Shouldn't still be riding that poor little thing. Miles too big for it ...' which was nonsense because Nutty's forebears had carried full-grown men across Dartmoor since the Ice Age and anyway, Alice always dismounted between heats, as much for her own comfort as Nutty's.

In only one respect did she fall short as the ideal child's first pony, as my mother discovered when buying her. For months she had gently tried to persuade the previous owner to part with her, but only just before the price was finally agreed did the curiously reluctant seller reveal Nutty's dark secret: she was not safe in a field with small children, and would kick them if she got the chance. Before the sale went through, my mother had to promise that she would never send a child alone to catch her.

There had, it seemed, been an incident involving broken ribs and a seven-year-old put off riding for good. Indeed, Nutty habitually laid back her ears and presented her hindquarters in

a menacing way even when an adult approached with a halter, and though she never wore shoes no one relished the prospect of being lammed in the shins by those hard little hoofs. Sweet talk and something delicious in the form of carrot or apple were needed to bring her head round towards you, but the moment the rope was round her neck she could be safely handled by a four-year-old.

She and Preciway made a strange pair. Once when I had a puncture on the M4 and was struggling with the wheelbrace, a Good Samaritan in a sports car spotted the horses fidgeting on the hard shoulder and screeched to a stop beside us. We were in a precarious situation. The puncture was in the Land Rover's back wheel, but I couldn't use the jack without unloading the trailer for fear of breaking the hitch, and in any case wasn't strong enough to shift the wheelnuts, which some demon of a mechanic had done up extra tight.

Nannie – not one of Nature's horse-lovers – was holding Preciway at arm's length, while Nutty, with Alice only lightly in charge, guzzled the grass on the bank. If either of them got loose on the motorway, we would have been in the soup.

Never have I felt such a surge of relief as when the stranger jumped out and said: 'Let me do that. Where's the jack?'

It was plain that he was in a tearing hurry, which made his action in coming to our aid all the more noble. In a twinkling he jacked up the Land Rover, changed the wheel, looked at his watch, and said, 'Must dash, I'm in the first race at Chepstow. Can you load the mare and foal yourselves?'

Given their relative sizes, it was a natural mistake. I assured him we could, popped Precy and Nutty back into the trailer and went on our way with a prayer of thankfulness and heartfelt hope that he would win every race he ever rode in.

Preciway lived with us for six years and was a hard act to follow. When hunting fit he was a splendid sight, his bright bay coat rippling with muscle. So long and smooth was his stride that you felt he was hardly moving and wondered why other horses couldn't keep up. My sister Olivia's vivid description of flying wired-up hedges, tigertraps and a five-barred gate on him during the best run of the 1970 season is the highlight of my Hunting Journal.

Only a thickened near fore remained to hint at past leg problems, but thoroughbreds are delicate creatures and since the Chilterns abound in flints sharp enough to puncture the sole of a hoof, we all gained a good deal of experience in poulticing and bandaging and spent much time crouching in the straw winding Animalintex and gamgee round his feet. It was tendon trouble, however, that did for him in the end. Veterinary bills mounted after a final injury, and reluctantly we took the decision to put him down.

Most of the equipment in the tackroom that relates to horse-breaking and training date from the era of his successor, who was a bit of a come-down in every sense. Long reins, lunging headcollar, roller, side-reins, mouthing-bit with little keys, long, snaky lunging whip and bits of many different shapes were all tried and rejected during the years when I tried unsuccessfully to school her to follow in his footsteps, but you can't make a silk purse out of a sow's ear, and though she eventually became an agreeable hack, Twiga was never going to rival Preciway.

Offspring of a spindly thoroughbred mare and a strapping Welsh cob sire, she was unfortunate in her physique. I had hoped for thoroughbred quality combined with Welsh cob sturdiness – quality leavened by substance – but the cross produced precisely the wrong result: a heavy Welsh cob body on fragile thoroughbred legs.

To add to her troubles, the foal was orphaned at birth, and she survived her rocky start in life entirely due to my parents' determination and resource. She was born in Wales, without much apparent difficulty, but after foaling, the mare didn't even try to get to her feet, and when my mother telephoned me at Bromsden to announce her arrival, she already knew something was seriously wrong. By the time I had driven from Oxfordshire, the mare was paralysed, the vet was mystified, and it was clear to us all that she was dying.

It was a hot, sultry July afternoon, buzzing with horseflies in the small paddock they had put her in for privacy, right under the windows of the house, and it was heartbreaking to see how the foal kept nuzzling and pawing with her small hoof at her recumbent dam, then lifting her head to search vainly for the teats that should have been above her.

'We'll have to bottle-feed her,' said my mother, but at once we hit a problem. At the time the only source of powdered mare's-milk was an Irish company, and owing to a postal strike supplies were not being delivered. Sow's milk was the nearest substitute, but not suitable for a new-born foal.

Presently the mare breathed her last, and we removed the

orphan to a stable as the threatened thunderstorm broke over the valley. Nutty had a foal of her own that year, and for an hour we tried to persuade her to allow the hungry orphan to suckle, but small as she was, she defeated all our efforts. Even with her hind legs tied together to stop her kicking, and her head held by two strong men to prevent her buffeting the usurper, her squeals of fury whenever we manoeuvred the poor foal close to her udder frightened it too badly for it to concentrate on the job. Nor would she let us handmilk her. Rigid with resentment, she held up her milk so that not a drop reached the basin, while with every minute that passed, the orphan grew weaker.

'Isn't there a kind of Foal Bank?' my father said, gazing over the half-door at the dejected foal. 'I'm sure I've read about it somewhere.'

A call to the British Horse Society confirmed it. Not long before, Miss Johanna Varden had set up a Foal Bank specifically to address problems like ours and put the owners of bereaved mares in touch with orphaned foals and vice versa. It was exactly what we needed, but would she have a match?

For three anxious hours we waited for her to ring back, while the foal lay in the straw, a pathetically angular collection of joints with clapped-in sides in a blackish covering, with a curious yellow fuzz on her saddle area. Although it was steamily hot, she began to shiver, so we bundled her up in a cellular blanket with a duvet over it, but we could see her vital force diminishing minute by minute.

At last the telephone shrilled: good news for us, but terrible for the teenager whose precious five-week-old foal had broken his neck in a freak accident that morning. She had bought him a top-quality leather 'slip' – a tiny head-collar designed for foals – and by ill-chance its ring had caught on the bolt of the stable door when he stuck an inquisitive head over. He had pulled back, the strong, new leather held fast, his neck was dislocated and he died instantly. The mare was distraught, neighing continually;

the teenage owner in floods of tears, but Yes, they would allow her to foster our foal and they lived near Worcester.

We were lucky that it wasn't near York, but even so it took Daddy and Bill, the farm manager, two hours' driving as fast as the stock lorry could go to get there by six o'clock. While Bill skinned the dead foal, Daddy did his best to console the owners.

'I'm afraid she's a bad traveller,' said the girl's mother apologetically. 'Just as well you didn't bring a trailer because she won't go into those at any price.'

As it was it took five of them and the stable broom to load Shamrock, frantic with stress and loss, and once in the lorry she flung herself from side to side, rocking the whole vehicle. Daddy said it had been a terrifying drive. She was wild-eyed, dripping with sweat, her udder shiny-tight with unused milk, when she came stiff-legged down the ramp just short of nine at night, and her earsplitting neighing echoed round the yard.

We lifted the orphan to her feet, dressed her in the dead foal's skin, a gruesome sight with the over-large ears fitted over her head, and semi-carried her into Shamrock's stable, propping her in a corner. This was crunch time, our last throw of the dice. Would Shamrock take to her? She was a big, powerful Irish Draught mare and she had had a terrible day. If she chose to take it out on the foal it would be curtains. We stood back, holding our breath.

Shamrock stopped neighing and stared for a long moment. The foal stood hunched up, head hanging, and did not move when sniffed and whiffled in a questing, rather peremptory way. The ill-fitting skin flopped sideways, dangerously close to coming adrift. Was Shamrock fooled? The foal may have smelled right, but it was nothing like her own.

Then a wonderful sound burst out from deep in her chest, more of a rumble than a whinny, and she gave the foal a gentle nudge, urging her round into a suckling position. Now it was up to the foal. Was she strong enough to respond to the signals?

Would she risk putting her head near a stranger after Nutty's furious squeals? Her nose rose, seeking blindly here and there, while Shamrock nuzzled her tail, willing her to take hold, find the teat...

The suspense was unbearable. I made a move towards them, longing to help, and was stopped in my tracks by Mummy's fierce headshake. *'Leave them alone!'*

Just as the foal looked ready to collapse and our nerves were stretched to breaking-point, her small black muzzle fastened on the teat, lost it, found it again, and at once she began to suck so noisily that we all exhaled in a whoosh of relief.

'Bingo!' whispered Daddy, and Bill silently stuck up his thumb.

Under our eyes, the foal seemed to expand. She lost her crumpled, defeated look, braced her legs, and wiggled her little bottle-brush of a tail, and never from that moment on did Shamrock show her anything but the tenderest care. It really was a miracle.

One large worry remained. Like all newborns, a foal needs colostrum from its first feeds to provide immunity from disease and infection, and since Shamrock had long exhausted her supply the vet decreed that Twiga, as we named the orphan because of her giraffe-like yellow-and-black coat, should not be allowed to get wet until she could build up her own resistance to disease.

Easier said than done during a typically rainy Welsh summer. The result was that, for the whole of the next year, whenever storm clouds gathered over the farm, whoever was nearest would hastily put a feed in the manger, then rush out to catch Shamrock and lead her into the stable, with Twiga skipping alongside. They both much enjoyed this routine, and the foal became very tame and well-disposed towards the human race.

Over the next four years, she accepted quite equably the succession of saddle, bridle, and human on her back, but she

had an independent streak and was inclined to question orders
before obeying them.

'You can't *really* expect me to do that?' she seemed to
be saying when required to walk through a puddle or jump
coloured bars. 'Look, there's a perfectly good way round.'

In many cases, I had to agree with her. Trotting and cantering
in small circles is an integral part of schooling a youngster, but
she found it boring and so did I, and this skimping of the basics
no doubt contributed to her unpredictable behaviour at low-level
riding-club competitions and in the hunting field. The ability
to hop over any obstacle that crops up is an important feature
of foxhunting, but though Twiga could jump like a springbok
when it suited her, I could never tell whether she was going to
take off or stop short in the last stride, and this led to some very
public disagreements between us. It was in no way Twiga's fault,
and her top-heavy physique didn't help.

At the first Meet I took her to, she bucked nonstop with
a curiously sedate rocking-horse movement – back and forth,
up and down – that soon had me and everyone else in the
vicinity helpless with laughter. On another occasion when
hounds checked during a brisk morning run, she lay down in a
muddy woodland ride and rolled with blissful abandon. I barely
had time to scramble clear, and was obliged to borrow a long-
thonged whip to get her to her feet again.

One way and another, she was never going to be the pride
of the South Oxfordshire or any other Hunt, and her later career
as hack for weekenders was much better suited to her talents.

Other horses came and went in the ensuing years, each
with its own quirks, physical and behavioural. An International
High-Goal polo pony who came to see out his retirement with
us used to spend the first five minutes or so after he was turned
out to graze cantering with short, smooth, grass-cutting
strides some thirty yards along the fence, whipping round at
the corner post and cantering back in the other direction, for

all the world as if he was practising his footwork.

Zorzal had been bred in the Argentine, and had a chestnut coat of such satiny perfection that it looked like burnished bronze, with the kind of green-and-purple iridescence that you see on a starling's head, but this smoothness made him vulnerable to midge attack on summer evenings, and he had evolved his own method of dealing with the nuisance. First he would plunge his head right up to the ears in the water-trough and splash it back and forth until great waves sloshed on to the ground and the whole area was liquid sludge. Then he would carefully roll in this mud-bath until he was coated all over in grey armour. The only way to get him clean was to run the hose over him, then scrape off the residue while he squirmed with pleasure, presenting different facets of his body to be worked on just like a man enjoying a massage.

Another chestnut, this time a home-bred yearling named Red Crescent, proved extraordinarily adept at letting himself out of his stable, and day after day I found him raiding the feed-shed next door to his box. Careful inspection of his mouth revealed that his tongue was split at the side, giving him a small thumb-like projection which he could fasten round the door-bolt and slide it open.

When asked if this would be a liability when we came to put a bit in his mouth, and the vet shook his head mournfully. 'Oh dear!' he said, deadpan. 'I'm afraid he'll always speak with a lisp.'

Even when Duff managed to negotiate squatters' rights over a strip of field on the other side of the garden, space was tight and grazing chronically scarce. Horses are wasteful feeders, preferring to nibble the shortest, sweetest sward and not only ignore coarse grass and weeds but deposit their droppings among them in such a way that even the most carefully managed pasture becomes progressively more depleted and sour.

To counter this, I took to buying a couple of ten-month-old

bullocks with robust appetites every year from my sister-in-law, partly to clean up the paddocks and partly to secure a supply of home-reared beef, but even they were daunted by the docks that infested the ground. We cut them, we dug them up, we even resorted to burning them off with a flame-thrower, but still they flourished.

'You'll never get rid of them without Gramoxone,' warned a visiting estate agent. 'Haven't you heard that a single dock seed can live *a thousand years?*'

It was depressing news. The last thing I wanted was to spray herbicide on our only patch of pasture. Like it or not, we would have to live with the docks.

Other creatures that were not strictly necessary kept joining the strength: some of whom turned out to be more congenial companions than others. The pair of geese I gave Duff for his birthday soon made themselves a nuisance by terrorising the dogs and leaving large green droppings on the lawn – a menace for the bare of foot – but there was something noble about the way the gander guarded his mate, standing sentinel at the door of her coop when she began to brood.

Hissing and flapping, he was formidable when challenged, so though I thought the eggs were taking a very long time to hatch, I didn't want to excite his wrath unnecessarily, and waited over a month before investigating the nest, only to find the goose still sitting but stone dead, stiff and cold inside the coop, her eggs devoured by rats or squirrels. Did the gander know? Before I could decide whether he was a tragic hero keeping vigil over his dead mate or simply very unobservant, the fox passed by and carried him off.

The peacocks, however, were an unalloyed success – at least while we lived at Bromsden. Surrounded by tall beeches and high-gabled barns, with no neighbour nearer than half a mile, it was the ideal place for them, providing plenty of wild food and safe roosting. Though ground-nesting and therefore vulnerable to foxes during the breeding season, so beautifully camouflaged were the peahens and so close did they sit among nettles and brambles that a human could almost tread on the nest before seeing it, while other predators could not apparently detect any scent while they were brooding.

We bought the original trio – Shalimar the peacock and two wives – from the director of a research project into peafowl then taking place at Nuneham Courtenay, and confined them in a pheasant-rearing pen for a fortnight before cautiously releasing them one by one over the next week. This slow acclimatisation is essential, we were told, and it worked very well, with the captive birds providing an inducement for the free one to stick around until all were 'hefted' to their new habitat.

It gave an exotic dimension to the farm to see them float gently down from their roost in a tall beech, and pace grandly about the yard and garden. Occasionally they would behead a flower or take a dust-bath in a newly raked seed-bed, but on the whole their splendour outweighed the damage to our plants, and Shalimar's stately ritual *pavane* before he shook out his train with a rippling rattle was a never-failing entertainment for the children.

The trio were early risers and saluted the dawn with a noisy chorus of screeches in summer, which brought back happy memories of the Indian jungle both for us and for Nannie who, in her twenties, had worked for the manager of a copper mine, and very much approved of the subcontinent and its peoples.

Ten years later, though, it was a different story when we moved to a new home in Gloucestershire – the home of my dreams, but unfortunately a good deal less suitable for peafowl because we had a near neighbour. He was an exceptionally kind and tolerant man, too deaf to worry about the screeches at dawn, but he loved his garden and even his forbearance did not extend to allowing peafowl to destroy his vegetables, nipping off the leading shoots of his peas and taking dustbaths in his young carrots.

It was painful to see him blaspheming and dancing with rage when he discovered his carefully tended plot transformed into a pot-holed mini Passchendaele.

'I'll shoot the brutes!' he roared, and it was in vain for me to promise to keep Shalimar and his ladies on our side of the buildings when with one flap of the wings they could sail over the intervening roofs and land on his lawn.

Another of this neighbour's loves was his big, old-fashioned Rover, which he kept in showroom condition despite the muddy lane, and his fury was understandable when Shalimar attacked his own reflection in its shining bonnet. Not only did he spatter it with blood, but with beak and claws he inflicted deep scratches which required expert attention from the garage. It became ever more clear that I would have to find the birds a new home.

Peafowl are not everyone's cup of tea, but to my surprise we found an immediate taker, an old friend who lived near Oxford, and kept purebred chickens as a hobby. She wanted Shalimar and his by-now extensive family. I wanted to part with them: it seemed the perfect arrangement. I went over to inspect their new habitat, and could see only one thing wrong with it. There were no tall trees near at hand. The farm was in a wide valley bottom, with the land rising gently about half a mile away on either side, and round the house the orchard trees looked barely high enough for peacocks to roost safely.

During the acclimatization period their new owner planned to keep them in an open-fronted barn wired in with chicken-netting, and I gave her the usual warning to let them out one at a time to accustom them to their surroundings. With some difficulty we captured three hens and two young cocks, but Shalimar himself evaded us.

'Never mind,' said Marika, transferring the bulging sacks to her car. 'Perhaps he can join us later.'

Three weeks later she rang to report trouble. The birds had looked so droopy and depressed after a fortnight's captivity that she had let them all out together, whereupon they had flown away in a flock and settled in the churchyard of the nearest village, a couple of miles away. She had put up notices in the village, asking residents not to feed the peacocks, in the hope that they would return when they got hungry, but even before she got back to her car she found her notices being torn down, and within days the village had split into two camps.

'They're our peacocks now,' declared one faction. 'These beautiful birds have chosen to live here. We must let them stay.'

'They are destructive pests. They'll ruin our gardens,' responded their opponents. 'Chase them away before they do any more damage.'

It was a difficult situation for Marika, but she would not admit defeat. With immense diplomacy she persuaded the more co-operative villagers to let her build traps in their gardens, baited them with peanuts and other favourite foods (raw pastry being a particular delicacy) and over the next three weeks she tried again and again to recapture the truants. At last – triumph! She lured all but one hen into her makeshift cage, and from a distance jerked the string that slammed the door shut. Her final move was to drive the captives over to Theale, near Reading, donate them to the Child Beale Trust, which specialises in exotic fowl and there, for all I know, their descendants may be living still.

On his own, with no hens to show off to or young cocks to challenge, Shalimar settled into a peaceful bachelor existence and ceased to torment our neighbour. *Cherchez la femme,* is the key to tiresome behaviour in most animal species – I do not exclude humans – and in his single state Shalimar gave us much pleasure yet even so, when he died at the age of thirteen, I did not replace him. Unless you live at least half a mile from the nearest household, Duff and I agreed it is best to leave peafowl in the Indian jungle where they belong.

CHAPTER FOUR

The Small Holding

IN THE LEAGUE tables of human stress, moving house is right up there with divorce and bereavement, but if leaving Bromsden was a wrench for me, it was far worse for Duff. Although I loved the house in its surrounding woods, deep down I had always been aware that it did not belong to us and never would. It was far and away the most covetable house on the two thousand-acre estate, and one day the owners were bound to want it back. When that day eventually came in 1985, it did not take me by surprise.

'What did Peter want?' I asked one spring morning as the land agent left after an unusually long session in Duff's study, and I added only half jokingly, 'Is he trying to turn us out of house and home?'

He didn't smile, let alone laugh. 'Well, yes,' he said after a pause. 'That's just about what it boils down to.'

So the blow had fallen at last, and though it may not have been wholly unexpected by me, it was very different for him. Bromsden had been his childhood home as well as the house where he brought up his own family. He knew every tree, every path, every rutting stand for deer and rough corner where a pheasant might be lurking, as well as every inch of the garden and buildings. He knew everyone who worked on the estate and had grown up with the locals. He had played cricket for the village and run the Shoot, built fences and mowed lawns, installed central heating and improved the house out of all recognition. It was very much his patch, and being asked to leave was much more of a blow to him than it was for me.

Yet the break was not ill-timed. Our children had flown the nest, so there was no hassle over schools; Nannie was installed in a bungalow, and there was nothing to stop us taking our animals to a new home, although we knew that finding anywhere comparable would be near impossible. Handsome brick-and-flint farmhouses don't grow on trees and South Oxfordshire – the first bit of real countryside outside London – is a very expensive area.

So where should we go? North, South, East or West? At the time it scarcely seemed to matter. We drew a circle that took in all the country less than two hours from London, and reluctantly began the disillusioning task of skimming through estate agents' brochures; but as it happened, finding a house did not take long. After visiting two in our price range that were poky, uncomfortable, cramped and dislikable in every way, a very small ad in the *Daily Telegraph* caught my eye, and two days later we drove to the western side of Gloucestershire to look it over.

It was by no means love at first sight when we left the narrow lane and surveyed the building set a few steps above a brashy farmyard. Built in Cotswold stone of several different vintages, with some brutalist grouting outlining the newest bits, the old house was long, low, and curiously proportioned, as if it had shrunk and expanded with the changing requirements of a succession of owners. It had, perhaps, started off as two cottages plus a barn, linked together with more regard for utility than aesthetics and, as we later learned from a neighbour, in 1936 the whole roof and top storey had been arbitrarily sliced off, because the weight of the heavy Cotswold stone roof was crushing the rest of the house, driving the walls outwards. Large metal cross-ties had then been driven through the first floor from side to side to lock the walls in place, and the roof replaced with ugly concrete tiles which didn't even project over the guttering.

It was, as the neighbour remarked, 'A proper farmer's job.'

The thick walls bulged, the mullions over the windows were fractured, and these were randomly placed where they cleared the metal cross-ties. It was easy to see why the estate agent's photographer had found it difficult to settle on an attractive angle for the brochure pictures. The whole property had a battered appearance, reinforced by crumbling stone walls round the garden and yard, against most of which wooden poles and long branches were propped to dry for firewood.

We exchanged a glance. 'No central heating,' I murmured.

Nor was there. But the stone-flagged kitchen was warmed by a four-oven Aga, and smelled of coffee and fresh-baked bread, and though most of the rooms were small and low-ceilinged, there was a large sitting-room with a handsome wooden floor and a wide stone hearth in which was set a wood-burning stove exactly like the one we had installed at Bromsden.

The atmosphere of benign neglect extended to the garden, fields and outbuildings. Only some fourteen acres remained of the hundred or so that the farm had owned in the 1930s, but in my eyes this was enough and to spare. What did it matter that the pasture was thick with buttercups and, on the banky field below the wood, nettles and thistles flourished in rank, head-high grass; that gates sagged on their hinges, the fences were a rusty tangle, and the one big barn was waist-deep in musty hay?

'It'll do,' we agreed, driving home. Two months later, after the briefest of negotiations, we had bought it and were planning our move.

Merciful oblivion now obscures most details of the three-day horror of packing up and moving the mass of furniture, livestock and equipment we had accumulated over twenty-four years. It was late in the autumn and seemed to rain continuously as we shuttled back and forth on the M4. We first transferred Nutty, the Dartmoor pony, as being the least likely to break through the little farm's vestigial fences then, leaving me to follow with the horses in my sister-in-law's lorry the next day, Duff extinguished the boiler for the last time and drove to Gloucestershire with his dog, the Land Rover stuffed to bursting, and a trailer full of screeching hens and peafowl.

Arriving after dark in pouring rain, his heart sank as he realised that he had left the key to the new house behind, and would have to break in. He opened the back and let out the dog, who ran a few steps towards the house, widdled briefly, and jumped back into the vehicle, her demeanour saying as clearly as if she had spoken, 'OK, that's enough of this place. Now let's get back home.'

But this place *was* home now. It was a bleak moment. As he sat in the dark car, wondering what to do first, a torch-beam came flickering towards him, and he slid open the window.

'You don't know me,' said the man with the torch, 'but I'm your new neighbour. That's my house over there, backing on to your yard. It struck me that you might be tired and hungry, so I took the liberty of cooking a second supper, and thought you might like to join me.'

Talk about the kindness of strangers! A strenuous hour later, after unloading the fowl and breaking into the house through an upstairs window, Duff was feeling more dead than alive as he walked the few steps down the lane and found Bernard's house warm and welcoming.

'Perhaps you'd like to ring your wife while I put the things on the table.' And as Duff sat at the telephone, reassuring me that he had arrived safely, a hand came over his shoulder to deposit a very large, very brown whisky and soda at his elbow. It was the start of a long and harmonious friendship.

Bernard Braithwaite was a county court judge on the western circuit, whose long experience of human villainy had not, miraculously, extinguished his faith in human nature. He was a lifelong bachelor, in earlier days a keen yachtsman and rider to hounds, gregarious and cheerful by nature, and socially much in demand. He at once took us under his wing and introduced us to his friends, which considerably softened the blow of leaving Oxfordshire, and many a happy evening did we spend in his company, one side of the yard or the other.

The field attached to his house had formerly belonged to a couple who had erected seven very large glasshouses, in which to grow carnations on contract for the Cunarders *Queen Mary* and *Queen Elizabeth* but, since the strip of ground faced north, the heating costs must have been astronomical even in the days of cheap fuel oil. Whether the business folded because the marriage failed or it happened the other way round is unclear, but the result was that when we arrived nothing but the skeletons of the last two glasshouses were still standing, roofless, and filled with tangled brambles, nettles and ash saplings.

The remains of all the others had been ruthlessly bulldozed to the edges of the field, where they formed a higgledy-piggledy redoubt of concrete blocks, shattered window-frames, metal reinforcing rods, and cats'-cradles of barbed wire – a truly horrible dump. To make matters worse, the entire field was carpeted with broken glass, so no animal could graze there in safety. It was an agricultural nightmare, but for the moment it was Bernard's headache, not ours, and he ignored it as far as possible by allowing Nature to take over in a mass of tangled greenery.

Though practically devoid of fences, the pasture in our own three fields just the other side of a ragged hedge was in better order, and after twenty-four years of eking out my grazing, almost to the point of counting blades of grass, I was in seventh heaven to have five whole hectares to accommodate my livestock.

The long bank that ran the full length of our territory on the lower edge of a steep wood we named Top Field; this was ideal summer grazing for sheep and, being dangerously precipitous, had never been cultivated. In its old turf were the deeply indented remains of a cart-track running diagonally across to the top corner, showing the original route of the road to Tetbury. Just beyond the gate at the far end, inside the wood, was the cavernous entrance to a badger sett – really a badger city – with countless pop-holes and secondary exits stretching deep into the hill. A white terrier bitch belonging to a neighbour was last seen heading for the sett's main entrance not long after our arrival. She never returned home, and there is no doubt in my mind that she encountered Brock below ground and was summarily despatched by those great grinding jaws.

Below Top Field stretched the big triangle known as Nichol's Piece which provided the cream of our grassland. As a parting goodwill gesture, our predecessor had provided for it to be ploughed and reseeded with a long-lasting mixed ley, which included useful varieties such as red and white clover, timothy and fescue. Because the last small field had originally been an orchard, a few surviving stumps lurked amid the docks and thistles which infested it, and rusty barbed wire of many vintages was stapled to a mixed bag of posts – round, rectangular, thick and thin – of which many were snapped off at ground level and held upright by the wire alone. This suggested more than the field's fair share of livestock breakouts.

Our most urgent task was to re-fence the entire property using squared sheep netting with two strands of barbed wire on top, expensive but necessary, and very fine it all looked when the job was complete. The deep rich loam washed down from the escarpment over many centuries made post-driving an entirely different affair from the back-breaking chore it had been in the Chilterns. Instead of having to excavate flints from clinging clay before the crowbar could penetrate the ground, here a couple of downward drives followed by a rotating movement would give you a hole so deep that you risked losing too much post below ground level.

There was a downside, of course. There always is. Posts that go in easily come out with just as little effort, and we soon discovered that fencing our fields was like repainting the Forth Bridge – no sooner completed than the first section required attention again. Only when the whole property was stock-proof did we consider acquiring farm animals, and naturally enough our thoughts turned first to cattle.

In the 1980s, before the successive plagues of Bovine Spongiform Encephalopathy (BSE or Mad Cow Disease) and Foot and Mouth Disease (FMD) ravaged the national herd and left a legacy of tight regulation and frequent ministry inspections, it was perfectly possible to rear a few calves for home consumption with minimal hassle from bureaucracy. You bought the weaned calves in spring, introduced them carefully to grass, then watched them grow to a suitable size before taking them in a trailer to the local butcher's abattoir. He would, for a fee, hang the meat in his chiller, then cut it into suitable joints, and hey, presto! you – and probably your nearest and dearest as well – had a freezer full of the best beef you could wish for.

Freezing it all before it went off was tricky. If the meat was piled in too quickly the temperature would rise, causing the plastic bags to clump together, which presented a problem when you wanted to get them out again. The whole operation could take 48 hours before everything was safely rock-hard, and I found it was as well to shuffle around the frozen contents so that we didn't end up with all the stewing beef at the bottom and mince at the top. No one wanted cottage pie four times a week because the cook couldn't find the fillet steak.

Home-reared beef is so very much more delicious than any you can buy that, despite the work involved, we persevered in keeping our own steers for a few years, but the epidemic of Mad Cow Disease which took devastating hold on the national herd in the 1980s, forced us to abandon our cattle enterprise.

Bovine Spongiform Encephalopathy was caused by the disgusting practice of feeding cattle with a protein supplement made from the ground-up meat, bone and offal of other cattle or sheep, effectively forcing cannibalism on herbivores. This caused holes to develop in the brains of affected animals, which lost their sense of balance and slowly became paralysed.

Unethical though it was to feed meat derivatives to herbivores, it would have been safe, technically speaking, if the cattle and sheep remains had been sterilised at high enough temperatures to neutralise the particular proteins called prions which damaged the brains of the beasts which consumed them. With shameful – but typical – parsimony, however, cattle-feed manufacturers saved on their energy bills by rendering the material at lower temperatures. Seldom has there been a more false economy. As ever more cattle were affected, slaughtered, and sent for disposal as meat and bonemeal, the disease snowballed out of control, and the cost to British agriculture and the cattle industry was horrifying.

Between 1988 and 2003, more than 170,000 cattle in England, Scotland, and Wales contracted BSE. Over a million unwanted calves were slaughtered, and over two and a quarter million older cattle were killed, their remains dumped in landfill in case they harboured infection. It is not surprising that regaining public confidence in the safety of eating beef proved a long, hard slog.

Though BSE was primarily a disease of milking cows, who were fed the contaminated meal to boost their milk production, beef consumption plunged as pictures of stricken animals filled TV screens and made headlines around the world. One country after another banned imports of British beef, and the sale of offal and beef on the bone were banned in the UK. Cattle markets were closed; the movement of cattle was severely restricted; agricultural shows could not exhibit cattle, and the cost to the taxpayer was estimated at over £4bn.

It was a financial disaster for livestock farmers – a tragedy that could and should have been avoided, and a wicked waste of cattle, money, and food. It was a long time before countries such as France, whose livestock producers barely bothered to conceal their glee at the removal of British competition for world meat markets, could be coerced into accepting British beef again, and in many ways the consequences of the epidemic are still with us for, predictably, authorities in both Brussels and Britain responded with a flurry of new regulation.

One infamous rule forbade beef from any animal over thirty months entering the food chain, which meant that slow-growing breeds like Highland Cattle or Welsh Blacks had to be killed before they reached maturity. Another decreed that the spinal cord and thymus had to be removed from all carcasses and, to the dismay of many gourmets, it became illegal to sell certain specified offal.

Hygiene regulations were stringently tightened. Butchers were obliged to sell cooked and raw meat from separate counters, washing their hands between handling each to prevent cross-contamination, and abattoirs were ordered to undergo such extensive and expensive upgrades of washing facilities and alterations of layout before being awarded a licence that many small local slaughterhouses were forced out of business.

Instead of meat inspectors, fully qualified vets were required to attend at abattoirs while animals were killed, which added enormously to butchers' costs. Movement licences had to list in triplicate the departure location, times of loading and unloading and destination, as well as identify the livestock being transported, and the washing and disinfection of lorries and trailers before and after visiting the abattoir was strictly enforced.

Just one year of adhering to all these rules was enough to convince us that the carefree days of rearing and eating our own beef were gone for good.

There was, besides, another sound reason for abandoning cattle farming. Gloucestershire is, like most of south-west England, heavily populated by badgers, and the fact that bovine tuberculosis is rife in this area is no coincidence. Both species are susceptible to TB, and the question of whether badgers infect cattle or cattle infect badgers has never been satisfactorily resolved.

Even though we seldom saw them, their labyrinthine network of setts, their sliding tracks down banks and straight up the other side, their communal lavatories and scooped-out passages under fences gave their presence away, and keeping them separate from cattle was, in practical terms, impossible.

Badgers may look slow, but they can bundle along at a good speed and cover a lot of ground with their nocturnal foraging. They climb stacked bales, and ooze their way into silage feeders with ease. Their powerful paws and claws help them burrow under buildings, destabilising the foundations; but their greatest crime is to drip urine continuously as they move about, polluting the grass so that grazing cattle cannot avoid contamination from tubercular badgers.

Two owners back, we were told, this smallholding of ours had been much bigger, a proper farm with a flourishing dairy herd. They sold milk, and made butter and cheese in the stone-flagged, east-facing room which is now my kitchen; but all that ended when TB testing became compulsory, because every animal in their thirty-strong milking herd reacted positively and had to be slaughtered. Sick at heart, that owner sold up and emigrated to Australia.

In the past, farmers were free to kill Brock by any means they could – digging out, shooting, snaring, or poisoning – and there is no doubt that some very cruel methods were employed even by people who would never resort to badger-baiting. All that changed radically in 1992, when badgers became a protected species, and ever since then arguments for and against reducing their numbers in bovine TB hotspots have been raging, while the cost of compensation to farmers for cattle slaughtered because of the disease has climbed to frightening heights. In 2010-11 it cost the taxpayer around £90m in England alone.

Even if agreement could be reached between farmers and wildlife conservationists, implementing a cull of diseased badgers would be fraught with difficulty. For a start, who would carry it out? Each badger would have to be trapped and tested individually, which would require enormous resources in manpower, traps, and veterinary inspection, probably against a background of covert resistance and subversion. With their attractive striped faces and clumsy, toylike gait, badgers are instantly recognisable and much loved by the non-farming public. It is hard to imagine that a weekend walker who discovered a badger in a cage-trap would not immediately release it.

Badgers are nocturnal feeders, usually just glimpsed in the headlights as they trundled across the lanes in the dark, but the ones we did see in daylight were frequently in a bad way. Emaciated, and raw with mange, they would sometimes take refuge in our buildings, looking for a quiet place to die. Even the most fervent bunny-hugger who saw one in that condition might have agreed that a cull was called for, if only to put sick ones out of their misery.

One summer evening I sent a five-year-old grand-daughter into the woodshed where I knew that a hen had been laying, and wondered why she stayed in there so long. 'Any eggs there?' I called at last.

'No, Granny, but there's a badger...'

'Leave it alone. Come out of there at once.' I guessed what kind of a state it would be in, and sure enough it had hardly the strength left to snarl when Duff went to investigate.

Barring a radical cull, the best hope of re-establishing a healthy population would be wholesale immunisation by means of baited vaccine, but even then there would be the problem of over-population. Besides, the emergence and licencing of an effective vaccine is still at least four years off – four years in which many more cows will be slaughtered, beef and dairy farmers lose their stock, and it will be necessary to import even more milk than we do now from France, where badgers are regarded as vermin, and *The Wind in the Willows* is not a children's classic.

So we decided to forget about rearing beef for the table until a reliable vaccine against bovine TB became available and, as our first spring turned into summer with acres of luscious new grass crying out to be eaten, we turned our attention to sheep.

First came the question of choosing a breed. On such a small acreage it obviously made sense to concentrate on quality rather than quantity, and keep pedigree animals which could be sold for breeding rather than simply for meat. But which should they be? Horned or polled? Long-woolled or short? Large or small? White or parti-coloured? The British Isles is home to over sixty distinct breeds, as well as many crossbreeds chosen for the best points of their pure-bred ancestors, which confronted us with a real *embarras de richesses.*

Since the price of wool had been dropping since the 1960s, and shearing a very small flock was always going to cost more than the fleece was worth, we rejected the heavy-woolled Merinos and Suffolks, as well as the super-tough North Country breeds, such as the impermeably-coated, independent-minded Herdwick, leggy Cheviot, and weather-resistant Blackface. Even the silky-ringletted Cotswold sheep, which might have seemed the obvious choice given where we lived, I passed over as too high-maintenance, and the same went for Jacob's Sheep, with their quirky horns and oddly patched fleeces, the endangered Manx Loghtan, nervous and high-strung despite his immense curving horns and heraldic mien, and the tiny Ouessant, the Breton Dwarf, black all over and more like a toy than a sheep.

Gradually whittling down the choice, we settled at last on two possibles. One was a foreigner: the handsome, chunky polled Dutchman called the Zwartbles, blackish-brown with a wide white blaze down the face, plus very striking white stockings and tipped tail, and the other the only breed that never needs to be shorn, because it sheds what fleece it has when the weather warms up in June: the noble, Roman-nosed Wiltshire Horn. For several weeks I hovered between the two, but eventually the Wilt won out. For the apprentice shepherd there is much to be said for a sheep whose condition is easy to assess because it is not obscured by wool, and besides, they appealed to my eye – a point that sounds superficial but is actually quite important when you consider how much you are going to see of your chosen breed, both in sickness and in health.

With its small head, long neck and curving horns, blocky body and long slim legs, a Wiltshire Horn ewe may be mistaken at a distance for a particularly sturdy goat. In May and June the peeling fleeces look ragged and unkempt, and there is a strong temptation for the shepherd to speed the shedding process by pulling off loose sections by hand. But the animals know to a T just how much they need to keep warm until summer has fully arrived, and it is often July before their sleek, snowy coats have shaken off the last vestiges of winter's coarse, crinkly kemp. I have often been asked who has shorn them so beautifully, without leaving any ridgemarks from the clippers.

The Wilt's horns are less of a plus – in fact they are a perfect nuisance. A mature ram has a pronounced Roman nose and great sweeping double-curled horns which end in a saucy little sideways flick with a very sharp point. Over the long months of growing these formidable weapons, he learns exactly how much clearance to give them, and how to use them to maximum effect. They can, in fact, be dangerous to himself as well as his rivals, because sometimes they bend inward so close to his jaw that they restrict his grazing and cudding. When this happens, the horns must be sawn and rasped on the inner edge until they are clear of his jaw, a difficult job requiring a blacksmith's strength and accuracy. With a mask of metal moulded round his face to protect his eye, the ram will accept the steady rasping with surprising equanimity, though it is advisable to confine him in a race between sheeted hurdles to prevent any sudden movements.

Once I heard a terrible banging noise in the paddock, accompanied by strangled grunts, and found our ram had managed to hook his left horn through the bar dividing a metal trough in half, and in trying to free himself had manoeuvred the whole trough up and round the curl of the horn. He was galloping about, half blinded by his burden, falling over from time to time, and in a real panic. I could not catch up with him until he was nearly exhausted, but when he fell over, gasping and foaming at the mouth, I was just strong enough to pin him down with my knees and twist the trough round until the metal bar came free, vowing meanwhile that never again would I leave a divided trough in his field.

All this was far in the future, though, when my mother and I drove into the Midlands to buy my first ewe lambs. We had contacted a breeder whose sheep were regular prizewinners, and she led us to a small stable in which were three suitable candidates – well grown ewe lambs about five months old. As the door opened, they dashed into the farthest corner and stared at us defiantly, stamping their forefeet.

'Right, let's have a look at them,' said my mother, seeing I had no idea which to choose .

Getting close enough to examine them was no easy matter, even in that confined space, for they were both strong and wild. Though horns look easy grab-handles, taking hold of them is a mistake, for not only does it trigger a fighting reflex, but it may result in the horn breaking off, leaving a horrible mess of bloody jelly in its place. Sheep are best controlled by hands either side of the head, cupping the jaw and, if necessary, extending over the eyes. This restriction of vision has a wonderfully calming effect, but this I was yet to learn.

After a short struggle, however, we managed to establish

that two of the little ewes were correctly equipped with teeth, teats, and four sound hoofs apiece, but when it came to the third, distinguished by a noticeably pink nose, my mother shook her head.

'We'll just take the two,' she said.

Strong men were summoned, and my purchases lifted bodily into the dog-carrying compartment of her Subaru.

'Why didn't you want the third one?' I asked as we drove home.

'I thought it looked a bit off colour.'

She was right. Within a week both my new ewes had developed swollen pink noses and looked far from well. In some alarm, I rang their breeder to ask what was wrong.

'Don't worry, they'll be all right,' she said dismissively. 'Put some purple spray on their muzzles. That'll fix it.'

But what would it fix?'

'Orf,' said our neighbouring farmer, who numbered his flock in hundreds. 'Contagious Pustular Dermatitis, if you want the proper name, and a proper bloody nuisance it is. Oh, your little ewes are weaned. They'll get over it in a week. Trouble is, once you've got it in the flock, it's the devil's own job to get rid of it. The ewes carry it on their udders, see, and when the lambs suck they catch it, and later on they'll pass it to their own lambs.'

This was most unwelcome news. 'Can't I vaccinate against it?'

He wrinkled his nose. 'Well, you can, but even so you'll still get the odd case. For myself, I doubt it's worth it. Better let it take its course, but don't breed from lambs that get it.'

A bad start to establishing a pedigree flock. Gloomily I foresaw a long succession of ewe lambs condemned as useless for breeding. Should I complain and ask the vendor to swap them for others? I could see several objections to this. Who could say that the swaps wouldn't exhibit the same symptoms in due course? Besides, she might justifiably say that a deal was a deal and caveat emptor. She had sold them in good faith, and they had been healthy enough when they left her premises.

The immediate problem was to catch the pink-nosed pair and anoint them with purple spray. Again, easier said than done. Though they looked hunched and listless from a distance, lying down with heads nodding in a six-acre field, they came to alarmed life the moment we approached, and sped off to the far fence. They had no intention of being cornered in the farm buildings, and without a sheepdog it was hard to guide them in the right direction. Because they were stuffed with grass and uninterested in bribery by bucket it took me and Duff and several passing ramblers nearly an hour to secure them in a shed.

During that hot and bothered hour, I composed an urgent shopping list. Sheep hurdles with which to make pens. Interlinking sheeted hurdles of varying lengths. Sliding gates. A guillotine gate which you could raise and drop while standing behind the sheep. A drafting gate that swung from side to side, directing sheep into different streams. As when you buy a hamster, the cage costs far more than the animal, so the little ewes looked like costing us a pretty penny in assorted handling equipment.

While we waited for this cornucopia of metal to be delivered, I kept the young ladies in a confined space and anointed them daily, learning in the process rather more than I wanted to know about Contagious Pustular Dermatitis, aka Orf.

As the name suggests, it is a messy, disfiguring illness, caused by a virus related to shingles in humans, and readily transmissible to humans, too. Stress, as at lambing or weaning, provokes the eruption of small red pustules, mostly around the mouth and nose, and these can trigger a secondary infection as the pustules turn into crusty sores. Young lambs so afflicted find it difficult to feed, and their dams' teats develop raw splits and scabs, so painful that they kick their lambs away when they try to suckle. So the lambs starve, the ewes get mastitis, and the distressing cycle may end with the death of the whole family.

Nor is that the end of it, because as our neighbour had warned, the virus can hang about for years. Some sheep seem to have a natural immunity, while others succumb for no discernible reason, which is why – after a decade of vaccinating and selective culling – I decided to 'Close' our flock, and maintain the clean status we had achieved by keeping and breeding only from home-reared ewes, and this we have done ever since.

It was all a hassle which, as a novice shepherd, I could have done without, but there was a silver lining. In the course of their treatment, being fed and ministered to while confined in a pen, the two little ewes became very tame. Good old greed conquered their fear of humans, and thereafter a call and the shake of a few sheep-cubes in a scoop would bring them across the field at a gallop, shaking their heads naughtily, and 'pronking' in stiff-legged leaps like gazelles as they raced to be first at the grub – a charming if ridiculous sight.

I also took the opportunity to teach them to pick up their feet like a pony for trimming. This was more for my benefit than theirs, since I found the backwards heave-and-twist with which a proper shepherd manoeuvres his sheep into a sitting position quite beyond me. Regular hoof-trimming is an unavoidable chore, particularly when the ground is soft and wet. Like fingernails, the horn keeps growing, and if nothing wears it down, the sides of the hoof curl inwards, trapping dirt between horn and quick. This may easily lead to infection. When the sole no longer presses against the ground, it can start to rot, and suddenly the sheep will go dead lame, needing urgent treatment.

There is a certain satisfaction, though, in the immediacy of the cure once you locate the infected spot. First a wash, then careful cutting-back all round the sole will finally reveal the source of the trouble, though sometimes it takes so much prodding and trimming that you fear to cut any more. In these cases, the trick is to let the animal rejoin its fellows, then watch the way it distributes its weight when grazing or walking about the field. The stress of being treated is often enough to mask any lameness temporarily, sometimes to the degree that you can't tell which foot is the culprit.

In the field, however, a sheep will quickly resume the gait which hurts least, favouring heel or toe as the case may be and, once you have identified its location,and penned up the patient once more, a single snip of the foot-shears will reveal a pus-filled cavity and – usually – bring immediate relief. After that a wash, a blast of foot-rot spray, and after a few tentative steps as if wondering why the hoof no longer hurts, the sheep will trot away as if it had never been lame in the first place.

There are so many occasions when a single-handed shepherd has to get close up and personal with his charges that a degree of tameness is a blessing. You can't blame sheep for being wary of humans. They have a low threshold of pain, and a short check-list of all the nasty experiences they routinely suffer at our hands from birth onward – tailing, tagging, castrating, worming, vaccinating – reinforces their natural desire to keep as far from us as they can. Add to that their inborn knowledge that they taste delicious, and not only humans but every carnivore they encounter would like to eat them, and you can see why they resist being singled out from their fellows and subjected to close inspection.

Having a companion near at hand reduces the panic level in any sick sheep, and makes it easier to treat, but there is a fine line between tameness and over-familiarity, particularly in the case of ram lambs. A bottle-reared 'tiddler,' or orphan, inevitably becomes very attached to the human holding the bottle, and even after he is weaned will come racing for attention the moment he sees him or her set foot in his field.

At first this seems rather sweet. *Aaah! he remembers me*, you think soppily, and feel that it would be brutal, even treacherous, to chase him away. But at this point it is well worth being tough, because what a human might mistake for affection is nothing of the kind. To the lamb, you are merely a remembered source of food, and if you encourage his attentions without giving him what he really wants, he will feel entitled to take it from you by force. A determined butt from a ten-week-old lamb is surprisingly painful – one sympathises with the ewes, who are practically lifted off the ground when their twins feel the need for a quick suckle – and once your one-time tiddler realises he can push you about, he can quickly become a pest.

We learned this the hard way, though our first lamb, the bold Agamemnon, was no tiddler but a big single, born in a snowstorm on April 2nd, and from the start he showed unusual strength and vigour. I was very proud of him, and when he was weaned I spent a good deal of time grooming him and teaching him to lead for the local agricultural show. Come the day, he won his class and then the championship, and I was walking on air as we circled the showground in the grand parade, with rosettes on his noseband and a cup in my hand.

Since he revelled in attention and seemed well suited to life in the limelight, I entered him for other, bigger shows, but soon had to recognise that he was not top-class in any way except ring-craft. There he excelled. As other rams slouched resentfully at the end of a rope and had to be hauled into position before the judge, Ags marched at my side with as much confidence as a well-trained dog, and stood like a rock even when subjected to intimate inspection.

Before he was full-grown, his big curling horns were so well developed that I found it prudent to substitute a head-collar and lead-stick for the rope halter, in order to keep the nearer horn a safe distance from my thigh as we paraded, and his tendency to give me a sly biff accidentally-on-purpose became gradually more pronounced. The way he treated trees and fence-posts illustrated his insensitivity to pain. At a show, nothing scared him – bands, lorries, dancing diggers – he wove his way calmly through them, and strolled up and down the ramp of his trailer with complete unconcern. The downside was that he wasn't in the least scared of humans, either.

Experienced shepherds warned me to beware of him. One old stager went so far as to growl, 'Best way to handle a ram is to clout him over the head with a stick every time you see him,' but I wasn't going to do that to Ags. Anyway, by then it was far too late to change his attitude.

It became noticeable that although he was complaisance itself while being brushed and shampooed and led about, he grew restive the moment he was no longer the centre of attention. If I made a move towards climbing out of his pen after a grooming session, he would lower his great head threateningly, so I was careful not to stand directly in front of him, and reversed out of his royal presence without turning my back.

At three years old he was in his prime, and it was on the day when he had been invited to appear as an exhibit in the Rare Breed Survival Trust stand at a show that I realised he had become dangerous. Throughout the afternoon he had dozed or nibbled hay in his pen while passers-by leaned over to admire and pet him, and I was about to lead him away to the trailer when an interested couple began asking questions, while their small daughter stroked the back of Ags's head.

'Likes that, doesn't he?' said the mother, smiling fondly. 'Come on, darling, time we went home.'

Ags's eyes were half closed. There was nothing he liked more than being stroked, but the moment the little girl took her hand away – before she could even step back from the pen – he put in a ferocious charge.

BAM! His frontal bone struck the metal hard enough to bend it, and had the child's arm still been hanging over the bars, it would have been shattered.

The parents were indignant. 'That was vicious!' they

exclaimed, and I could not deny it. Clearly it was time the High King retired from public duties.

Do sheep suffer from boredom? As the old troop horse snorts at the sound of trumpets, and the hunter cocks his ears for the horn, did Agamemnon dream of loudspeakers blaring and the bustle of crowds?

Silly question. Nevertheless, it was tempting to suppose that the close interest he took in whatever we did in garden or fields stemmed from nostalgia for his glory days. As he entered his fifth year, however, it became increasingly plain that his intentions towards us were no longer benign. It was disturbing to find ourselves under constant surveillance from those yellow, unblinking eyes as Ags moved from one vantage point to another to make sure we couldn't slip past him unobserved.

If I went near his paddock to hang washing on the line, he would canter across and solicit petting, which would have been endearing had I not known that as soon as I moved away he would lower his head, take two quick steps backwards and one to the side, like a place-kicker, and charge at the fence where I had been standing. When Duff was mowing, Ags would pace along the fence parallel with the lawnmower, just as fighting stags march side by side before swivelling inward to lock antlers. When the machine was switched off, he would batter the gatepost until there was blood on his horns.

It wasn't that he lacked company. Three vastly fat, superannuated wethers, who had started life chez my niece as bottle-reared tiddlers and were now far beyond the butcher's knife, shared his paddock and took as little notice of us as we did of them, but Ags was always on the *qui vive*.

One dark, wet, February afternoon, when I was at my desk, gazing vacantly up the hill, I saw a white blur move swiftly on the footpath that crosses our top field. Seconds later, a dark shape flew through the air, struggled briefly, then crashed over the wire fence into the lower paddock.

I didn't see that, was my shameful first reaction; but there was no denying what had happened. Below the fence, a man was on his hands and knees, while above it Agamemnon stood glaring through the wire.

Pulling on boots, I ran outside. The victim was shaking all over and plastered in mud. In one hand he still held the fork he had been carrying on his way home from work in our neighbour's garden. He had a perfect right to be on the footpath, and must have been taken completely by surprise by Ags's swift charge. If he had used the fork to defend himself, he could have done the ram serious harm.

'Are you OK?' I asked anxiously, but the man seemed too shocked to speak. 'Come in. Have a wash. Have a cup of tea.' I tried to urge him towards the kitchen, but he wouldn't come.

'N-n-no! Want to – want to get home,' he gabbled, backing away, and scuttled downhill towards the village.

I watched him, thinking hard. He was more frightened than hurt, but next time we might not be so lucky. Two of our three fields are crossed by footpaths, so that put them out of bounds for Agamemnon in future. Our options for places to keep him were becoming extremely limited.

Another problem loomed – genetic, this time. All but one of our older ewes were unrelated to Ags, so he could continue to serve them, but by now the ewe lambs I had been retaining to increase the flock were his grown-up daughters. I needed a second ram, in order to run parallel bloodlines for the next two years, but how could we accommodate him?

'Put masks on them both,' advised an experienced shepherd. 'Just for a few days, until they get used to the smell of one another. After that you shouldn't have any trouble with them fighting.'

The new ram was called Rivet – a year younger and more lightly built than Ags, who had become very portly. The leather masks I bought fitted over the ears with a complicated arrangement of adjustable straps, and covered the cheeks and frontal bone halfway to the muzzle, tying under the chin. The eyeholes had sideways projections, like sticking-out blinkers, which blocked the view forward, making it difficult to aim a charge.

Neither of the rams seemed to resent this restriction of vision, and after circling and shoving each other a bit while we watched, ready to intervene at any sign of aggression, they settled down to graze alongside the three old wethers. As darkness fell, the group was lying together – a gentlemen's club – and we went to bed thinking all was well.

Peace reigned among them for a week, until by rubbing against a tree Ags managed to twist his mask sideways, so that he couldn't see out at all. I found him blundering about, bumping into things, so penned him and removed the mask. Afterwards – with difficulty – I did the same for Rivet, who was not used to being handled. Surely, I thought, they've been together long enough to know one another's smell?

Wrong. Next morning I could only see one ram in the paddock, plus the three wethers. Rivet had vanished. I thought he must have jumped the fence, but as we searched the thick hedge, something moved in the brambles where poor Rivet had been thrown or taken refuge. He was trying to rise, but his hind leg had been broken above the hock, and there was nothing for it but to shoot him on the spot.

Another very black mark against Agamemnon, and reluctantly I faced the fact that it was time for him to go. At the age of five, a ram's fertility declines, so it was unlikely I could sell him on, and in any case I would have to come clean about his psychological quirks. A bullet was the obvious answer, but from day to day we kept putting off the date of execution, until an unlooked-for solution presented itself.

A friend, who kept pigs and a few sheep in his orchard, had a German wife with a blunt, no-nonsense approach to livestock.

She had seen Ags at a show, and wanted him to serve her ewes. Yes, she was perfectly familiar with rams, and knew how to handle them. No, his reputation didn't worry her in the least. If we would bring him over in our trailer, she undertook to give him one last season of domestic felicity before taking him to the nearby abattoir.

It was only a stop-gap solution, and I can't say I was keen on it, particularly when they asked me to leave Ags in a former pigsty with a wooden gate while they went to fetch in the ewes. He climbed up with his forefeet on top of the gate, and I wondered how long it would withstand his charges.

Later that evening, we had a reassuring telephone call. Ags was fine. He had settled down well. They would put him out with the ewes in the morning.

Two days passed, and Jutte rang again. The ram was so friendly, so biddable. She didn't know what we were worried about. He came when she called. She could lead him about like a lamb .

'Well, yes,' I said. 'He's very good to lead. It's when you take the headcollar off...'

Another day, another telephone call. Jutte again. 'Please will you come and fetch your ram? Yes. Now. Immediately.'

We were just leaving to go out to dinner. 'Won't tomorrow morning do?'

'It is better now.' She sounded agitated. 'We can't wait all the night.'

'Why? What's happened?'

'He's got our neighbour up a tree.'

So the final throw had failed. When I rattled some cubes in a scoop, Ags came trotting away from his prey, and put his nose in the head-collar, ready for the journey home.

We gave him another month with his fat pals, and I asked my sister, the artist Olivia Stewart-Smith, to paint him. We tethered him between two strong posts, and he stood composedly while she started work on a frontal view, concentrating on his great head and noble, sweeping horns. Presently he grew bored, as sitters do, and leaned sideways, gently moving his right horn to and fro.

The artist worked steadily, and had already achieved a striking likeness when she realised that her subject was using the sharp inner edge of his horn to fray the head-rope. Only a few strands remained. She began to work faster.

'You can't have finished already,' I said, coming out with coffee and finding her folding the easel.

'I've got enough. I'll take a few photographs and finish it in my studio,' she replied, snapping away at a safe distance. Ags gave an experimental tug at his tether and, as the last strands parted, I understood the artist's haste.

The portrait was a great success. Outlined in strong brushwork against a clear blue sky, the ram's head with its curled horns menaces the observer, seeming about to charge out of the canvas. The artist has caught his split personality, too. One eye looks kindly, almost melancholy, its eyelid gently drooping, while the other fixes you with the cocksure, aggressive glare which foretold mischief.

As summer ended and the goodness went out of the grass, Duff finally put a bullet through Agamemnon's head, and I resolved never again to make a pet of a ram.

CHAPTER FIVE

Trials and Tribulations

EARLY IN 2001 another hammer blow struck British agriculture. This one was to bring not only farming life but also tourism and free movement within the countryside to a grinding halt. Once again it was triggered by dirty farming practice and illegal cost-cutting, and this time the scourge was the well-known, much-dreaded Foot and Mouth Disease (FMD), a highly contagious and easily transmissible viral infection which can affect a wide range of farm livestock: cows, sheep, alpacas and llamas, buffalo, pigs, and goats, as well as a variety of wildlife, with deer, rats, and hedgehogs being among the animals known to be susceptible to it.

The origin of this outbreak was traced to a run-down farm at Heddon on the Wall in Tyne and Wear, where the pigs had been fed with untreated swill from a local restaurant. The precise nature of the infective agent was never identified: most likely it was illegally imported meat from a country where the disease was endemic.

Because so many local abattoirs had been forced to close by the stringent and expensive regulations that came into force after the BSE epidemic, animals were routinely being transported long distances to slaughter. By the time the characteristic lameness and blisters in the mouth were spotted, the pigs from Tyne and Wear had travelled to a slaughterhouse in Essex, spreading disease all the way.

Nor had the contagion followed this route alone. Blown by the wind from the farm at Heddon, it infected sheep in fields nearby, and after these animals were sold in Hexham Market, stock-lorries distributed them far and wide throughout the country. Outbreaks flared with terrible speed along the north to south-west line of the M6 and M5, and to either side of it, taking in Anglesey, Herefordshire, Gloucestershire, Somerset, Devon and Cornwall.

In late February, 2001, we had just returned to the torrid turmoil of New Delhi after visiting Indian friends on the Indian-Nepalese border. As I idly flicked through newspapers for the first time in three weeks, a paragraph in the foreign news caught my eye: *FMD in England,* and bang went our peace of mind for months to come. I could still hazily remember how, during an outbreak in 1967, healthy animals had been compulsorily slaughtered and country activities suspended until it was stamped out. That had been limited to Worcestershire and the surrounding counties. This time even the initial reports made clear that it was far more widespread.

FMD is not necessarily fatal, and most affected animals would, left to their own devices, eventually recover from the lameness caused by blisters between the cleats or foot-pads and around the mouth, which make feeding painful. Leaving them to their own devices is not, however, an option. The disease is highly infectious and easily spread by breath and body fluids, borne on the wind, carried on boots, paws, wheels – in short, once established in a country it is extremely difficult to contain, let alone eradicate.

Both the Ministry of Agriculture, Fisheries and Food (MAFF), and the National Farmers' Union (NFU) – with whom they maintained an all-too-cosy relationship – were determined not to compromise Britain's status as a FMD-free country, or the flourishing export trade in meat and breeding stock, and to protect these they were prepared to slaughter enormous numbers of healthy animals as well as the comparatively few actually carrying the disease, simply because they were located near enough to the outbreak to be considered at risk.

But how near was too near? On neighbouring farms, or on the neighbouring farms to farms adjoining the farms where the disease had been confirmed? In a circle 3km in radius from the outbreak – or 5, or 10? Across a river, or the other side of a hill? It was difficult to decide, and as the disease progressed, new boundaries marking infected and non-infected zones were continually drawn – and scrapped – and redrawn, with restrictions of varying severity arbitrarily imposed by faceless bureaucrats and panicking politicians.

In some zones farmers were allowed to move livestock within its boundaries but not across them into the next zone. In others, even moving animals from field to field within a farm that spanned a lane was forbidden. March and April are hungry months, when last year's grass has been grazed to soil level, and new grass is barely showing. Muddy months, too, so the strict rules demanding disinfection of the wheels of every vehicle used to carry hay or silage every time it left the farmyard became a long-running nightmare.

Early spring is also lambing time, and many in-lamb ewes were still 'at tack,' ie boarded out in winter quarters for the last weeks before being brought into the home lambing-sheds. Desperate to get them under cover before they gave birth, some sheep farmers hired marquees in which to erect lambing-pens, and themselves lived in caravans on the tack-owner's fields in order to care for their ewes and lambs at this most vulnerable time.

Though the outbreak was still in its early stages, as we hurried home we realised how serious it threatened to be when we saw evidence of lock-down at every farm entrance we passed. Tubs of disinfectant and thick mats of soaked straw blocked gateways, with large official notices warning people to keep out, wash their boots, no dogs, no admittance, and we were glad to find that our friend Diana, who had looked after our livestock in our absence, had taken the same precautions and placed handwritten placards warning *Do Not Enter* on each of the stiles where footpaths crossed our fields. It was like entering a plague zone.

Day by day the news got worse and regulations proliferated. Ministry vets and Animal Health Officers dressed from head to foot in protective suits made surprise visits or insisted on blood-tests at short notice. From our worm's eye view at the very bottom of the farming chain, many of these tests with their accompanying forms and paperwork seemed not only useless but counter-productive.

Why was one team, which was led by a paper-suited, rubber-gloved and booted temporary inspector, who haled from the FMD hotspot of Dumfries and Galloway, sent to bring possible contagion to our nice clean farm? Why did he wear a hairnet but nothing to cover his bushy red beard?

'Ma beard's clean enough. Ah wash it evrra day,' he snapped when I mentioned it as a possible hazard.

'If you washed it in the disinfectant we've got at the gate, you'd have no beard left,' I retorted. It was rude, but we were all on edge.

I wasn't the only one to be suspicious of interlopers. Vets and inspectors were being recruited from all over the place and some hardly spoke English. As a result, xenophobia flourished. Walkers and ramblers were definitely non grata, and strangers with unrecognised car-numbers were instantly reported or warned off.

Nastier still were the rumours that some farmers were profiting from the catastrophe, even infecting their own livestock in order to claim compensation when they were slaughtered. No one could actually pinpoint a culprit, but it was an ugly possibility. People muttered that the NFU and MAFF were in cahoots in their efforts to drive small farmers out of business, and thus reduce the amount of subsidy they had to pay through the Common Agricultural Policy (CAP).

There was news every day of some fresh disaster, and television reports were dominated by gruesome footage, beamed into every living-room. The wholesale shooting of squealing pigs and terrified sheep; cattle, calves and new-born lambs lying in heaps in their own yards; farming families fighting back tears as the slaughtermen went about their grim work. Still more haunting were the images of foreloaders scooping up massed carcases to dump in trucks, which were then driven to burning pits where the tangled bodies twisted and blackened in the flames. A sickening sight, with seagulls swooping overhead, impossible to control as they spread the disease more widely still.

Restrictions grew ever tighter. Hunting stopped. Racing stopped. Sporting fixtures of every kind were cancelled. Footpaths were closed, so dog-owners were forced to exercise their animals on the road. The tourist trade was badly hit, and the many businesses connected with it faced ruin: hotels, B&Bs, gift shops, restaurants, riding schools and coach-tour operators.

The Lake District was officially declared closed, and in a stark illustration of the financial pain this caused, in a single March day one hotelier in the heart of the Lakeland Fells lost £35,000 worth of forward bookings. The General Election scheduled for April was postponed, but the Labour government was floundering, out of its depth, and in its ignorance of the way the countryside worked, it spread unnecessary alarm and despondency by making contradictory statements about which areas were, or were not, to be culled of all susceptible livestock, sick and healthy alike.

Few politicians seemed to have read the wide-ranging, meticulous report of the enquiry chaired by the Duke of Northumberland after the 1967/8 outbreak of FMD in the north-west Midlands, let alone implemented the report's many recommendations for dealing with a future epidemic. The painful result of official dithering and lack of effective organisation was that the backlog of slaughtered animals both infected and healthy constantly increased until the resources of the Ministry were overwhelmed. They had neither the manpower nor logistics to dispose of so many carcases.

Instead of bringing in the Army at once, as the Northumberland report had recommended, they muddled along piecemeal using civilian slaughterers, knackers, and hauliers to transport the dead animals to disposal points, falling even farther behind with the work.

When at last military personnel were ordered to assume responsibility for locating pyres and digging burial pits, and for transporting carcases, many of these were in an advanced state of putrefaction, and on farms where all the livestock had been killed, the family might have been marooned for a fortnight in their own house, surrounded by yards full of the rotting corpses of the animals that had been not only their pride and joy, but their livelihood as well.

It could be argued that sheep and cattle are in any case ultimately destined for the slaughterhouse and the epidemic merely hastened their end, but this haphazard, wholesale destruction of young and old, healthy and sick, common or pedigree stock, with no possibility of appeal or reprieve, was deeply shocking. Bloodlines that had been carefully nurtured for generations were wiped out in a day, and on top of the waste, horror and grief, the bloody-mindedness and bureaucracy of officialdom sickened everyone who came in contact with it.

Very early on in the epidemic it had become plain that Cumbria, geographically the centre of the United Kingdom, was also the epicentre of disease. The biggest livestock dealers regularly came to Carlisle for their cattle and Longtown for their sheep, and since large quantities of infective material carrying the FMD virus is shed before animals show any symptoms of disease, this year their lorries had been delivering beasts from the Cumbrian markets to all parts of the British Isles.

Maps showed a giveaway pattern of confirmed outbreaks either side of motorways, where sheep and cattle reared in the north of England had been transported for fattening to the better pasture of the south-west, and the knowledge that its main route of transit was no more than five miles from us did nothing to calm our fears.

As we grappled with buckets and haybales to keep all the animals fed in a long-drawn-out and very wet, cold spring, juggling the sheep, horses, and alpacas from one field to another and longing for the grass to get a move on and *grow*, I was thankful that we had only twenty ewes to lamb and enough sheds to get each of them penned and under cover when she decided to give birth. There was the usual sudden rush at the beginning, showing that the tup had been busy during his first few days of marital bliss; then production tailed off to a slow straggle, with nearly a month between the first-born lamb and the back-marker.

During that month we went out as little as possible. Confirmed cases of FMD on the banks of the Severn had brought the infection terrifyingly close. Worse, oozing truckloads of dead animals were being brought from infected farms further up the vale, and burned no more than three miles away as the crow flies. And the crows did fly – along with buzzards, seagulls, pigeons, and rooks – soaring along the rim of the Cotswold escarpment as they engaged in their usual spring business of building nests and scavenging for food, bringing who knew what traces of virus from the pyre to the rest of the valley?

The same applied to all free-ranging wildlife. What was the use of keeping beef and dairy cattle under lock and key in a covered yard when a disease-carrying badger might be urinating in the silage-clamp, or a fox drinking from the water-trough? Farmers in the neighbourhood were in total lockdown, rapidly running out of winter forage for their yarded beasts. Small wonder that the price of big bales doubled by mid-April, when the animals were usually turned out to grass.

As the months passed, the dilemma of what to do with beasts who, in the terms dictated by the BSE epidemic, had passed their Sell-By date, grew ever more acute. The Over Thirty Month (OTMS) rule stipulated that beef animals over that age were not allowed to enter the human food chain, since after this it was thought they might be old enough to develop bovine spongiform encephalopathy. It was a shamefully wasteful policy, which meant that slow-maturing breeds were effectively barred from the meat trade, (though eventually in 2005 the law was amended to allow cattle over 48 months to enter the food chain provided all tissue that might contain the BSE prion had been removed by the abattoir).

Night after night, the TV news was dominated by reports of fresh outbreaks of foot-and-mouth disease, with grim pictures of panicking sheep being chased by white-clad slaughtermen, of enormous blazing pyres, or tear-streaked children whose family farm had been served with the dreaded D Notice as the prelude to exterminating the livestock there.

Newspaper campaigns were launched to save particular animals, with varying success. Monks mounted a round-the-clock vigil to prevent the killing of a sacred bull belonging to a Hindu shrine, but eventually had to give in. By contrast, a pure-white Charolais calf named – inevitably – Phoenix, which was discovered alive several days after its mother and the rest of its kindred had been slaughtered, was reprieved by the Prime Minister after a public outcry – a triumph of sentimentality over logic.

Since the virus thrives in cold, wet conditions, everyone prayed for a heatwave, but it was not until late June that there was a noticeable diminution of confirmed cases, and only at the end of September that the last report of infection allowed the country to believe the disease was finally under control.

That was by no means the end of 2001's tribulations, however. Hated and despised throughout the seven-month epidemic for its officious incompetence and inertia, the Ministry of Agriculture, Fisheries and Food had morphed into a new body to be known as DEFRA – the elaborately named Department for the Environment, Food, and Rural Affairs – but since this new department was composed of many of the same civil servants who had formerly run MAFF, and exhibited just the same devotion to forms in triplicate, incomprehensible jargon and buck-passing as its predecessor, disgruntled farmers who had to deal with DEFRA pointed out that the changed name had no more impact than when Windscale nuclear establishment became known as Sellafield.

Cleaning and disinfecting affected premises was a long hard job which took months to complete. Wooden barn doors, feed troughs, and hayracks had to be ripped out and burnt, and hardcore removed from farmyards. Sales of power-hoses, disinfectants and pressure-washers soared as concrete barriers and plaster on walls up to the height of ten feet were scoured clean, but it was late in the year before FM7 forms denoting that all buildings, machinery and equipment were clean enough to satisfy DEFRA inspectors were issued to farms where livestock had been exterminated, and most farmers decided to leave any question of restocking until the following spring.

It was a grim, gruelling, gruesome year for anyone connected with animals susceptible to foot-and-mouth disease. During those seven months of countryside lockdown, the epidemic was estimated to have cost the taxpayer £8 billion. Six and a half million animals had been killed, though the number of confirmed cases was no more than 2026, stark figures which have re-ignited the argument for vaccination rather than wholesale slaughter in any future outbreak of FMD.

Even in the best of times, when there is no large-scale agricultural plague threatening livestock, I found it difficult to keep all the animals we had on the strength healthy all the time, and when the epidemic of 2001 was definitely over, we took the decision to reduce our headage to a more sensible level. Never again did I want to own more animals than we could feed or, if necessary, bring under cover without overcrowding.

It was hardly surprising that having spent twelve years in our former home scrabbling around for grazing, with no more than a rented acre and a half of poor, sour grass at our disposal, the possession of five whole hectares of excellent pasture had gone to my head. Year on year I had steadily increased the number of animals our fields were required to support. I had added extra horses from time to time, a couple of donkeys here, and a trio of alpacas there. Every season I had retained a few extra homebred shearlings until the flock numbered nearly fifty each summer, but the FMD epidemic had been a wake-up call, demonstrating how vulnerable to disease this overstocking made us.

During that long, cold, anxious spring I had lost several lambs through my reluctance to call out the vet from his premises so close to the nearest FMD outbreak. Who knew what invisible virus might be clinging to some part of his vehicle, no matter how thoroughly it was washed and disinfected?

Then there were the run-of-the mill injuries and illnesses to consider. With such a mixed bag of livestock, there always seemed to be at least one four-footed dependent giving cause for concern. A persistently lame ram. A donkey with a nasty cough. A horse who reacted so badly to midge-bites that she rubbed her mane and tail raw between May and September. Chickens with scaly eruptions on their legs, alpacas who became mysteriously lethargic, lay down, and quietly died – the list was never-ending. Few warranted an expensive visit from the vet, but one could spend a fortune on over-the-counter powders and lotions that seldom did much good.

Dealing with death is always distressing, but anyone who keeps animals has to get used to it. As with children, infections and injuries seem to come in waves, and since sheep are susceptible to an astonishing range of illnesses, not all of which can be cured by antibiotics, from time to time we would find ourselves in need of a way to dispose of large dead bodies.

At lambing time, in particular, many things can go wrong. The most common vicious spiral involves the malpresentation of lambs in a multiple birth, which leaves the ewe too exhausted to feed her family, or the lambs themselves too weak to suckle. That means the ewe will probably have too much or too little milk, which in turn may lead to mastitis, which may or may not respond to antibiotics, but all too often results in sudden death.

Quite apart from the difficulty of saving the orphan lambs, there is then an urgent need to dispose of the heavy, awkward, stiffening corpse. At seventy to ninety kilos, a full-grown Wiltshire Horn ewe is too big to bury or take to the local recycling plant, so when you have recovered from the shock of her death, the question is what to do with the carcase?

In the easygoing past, most fallen stock would be accepted by the local hunt. A telephone call to the kennelman would be followed by the prompt arrival of the flesh-van. The dead animal would be winched into its cavernous depths, a modest donation made to the hunt, and off would go the carcase to be skinned, cut up, and added to the hounds' diet.

Then came a period when hunts phased out such collections, partly because of cost, partly because of the fear of some infection and, in any case , getting a taste for mutton is bad for the morals of a hound which has been so carefully trained to ignore sheep on the hoof. The smallholder faced with a carcase to dispose of then had the option of burying on his own land – difficult without a mechanical digger – or persuading a larger farmer to allow it to disintegrate in his muck-heap, a course which put the owner of the dead sheep under a certain obligation and couldn't be exploited too often.

Presently even this option became impossible. Post BSE, post FMD, the rules governing the disposal of carcases became ever tighter. On-farm burial or burning was forbidden for fear of polluting water-courses, and the same went for allowing dead animals to rot in a muckheap.

Smallholders like us found ourselves in an impossible position, with no above-board means of disposing of fallen stock. It took an unpleasant spate of fly-tipping, when bloated sheep carcases – whose ears had been cut off to make identification impossible – were dumped beside roads or in lay-bys, to spur the Government into recognising the problem. At last in 2005, a not-for-profit organisation called the National Fallen Stock Company (NFSCo) was set up, and its existence has considerably improved matters.

Membership of the NFSCo gives access to a list of all the deadstock hauliers in the neighbourhood, and their collection rates for disposing of each category of animal. Instead of the unsatisfactory and guilt-inducing business of negotiating some hole-and-corner arrangement with a neighbour, a single telephone call will bring a clean lorry equipped with a winch and cheerful, competent collector to your farm within 48 hours. Although it doesn't make the loss of an animal any less tragic, it certainly removes much of the stress from the aftermath.

Smaller fatalities are all too common, and these have to be dealt with on a case-by-case basis. It is hardly worth summoning the fallen stock lorry for a stillborn lamb or suffocated piglet, still less for a chicken that succumbs to coccidiosis or old age. Here scavenging foxes, badgers, ravens and carrion crows still have a useful part to play. Once a creature is definitely dead I am not squeamish about disposing of it, but in common with most women I am bad on the in-between cases, and find it difficult to administer the *coup de grace* even when it is plainly the kindest thing to do. Using the right degree of force to break the neck of a diseased hen without pulling its head off, or to kill a moribund rabbit without getting covered with blood are practical skills necessary to every smallholder, and I am very fortunate that my husband has these at his fingertips.

CHAPTER SIX

The Shepherding Year

Although I have now been keeping sheep for quarter of a century, I still have much to learn about breeding, rearing, and finally selling them, for every year brings its own challenges, many of them relating that notorious imponderable against which every farmer complains unceasingly – the weather. Whatever it throws at us is always going to be wrong for someone. A dry cold winter with a warm wet spring produces a completely different set of problems from a mild winter with late frost and snow, but once the reproductive cycle is under way, the ewes will give birth whatever the weather conditions, whether there is enough grass to support them or not, and all the shepherd can do is hope for the best while providing for the worst.

Midway between the shortest day and the Spring equinox, Candlemas Day – February 2nd – tends to catch me by surprise. By tradition, at that point in the winter a farmer should have used up no more than half his supply of forage, whereas by then I am usually down to my last few bales.

The shepherding year begins, as the calendar year ought to, when summer gives way to autumn. Surveying our fields with their September glut of long, lush grass, I have to cast my mind back to those bleak days in 2001, when it seemed as if winter would never end, and every blade of green was nipped off level with the mud the moment it appeared, in order to counter the temptation to add just a few more sheep to my little flock.

Enticing schedules for the big autumn sheep shows-and-sales up and down the country are best binned immediately, lest my resolve weakens – though in every third or fourth year, when we are in need of a new ram, I usually trawl through the *Private Sales* columns on the Wiltshire Horn Society website, to see what is on offer and compare prices and bloodlines. As with all minor breeds, the gene pool is relatively small, so it makes sense to breed from stock unrelated to our own for several generations.

Meantime, the weather is changing, and with it the behaviour of the sheep. As the days shorten and the temperature drops, even the most stately ewes become skittish, engaging in sparring matches or rushing headlong from one end of the field to another for no apparent reason.

At the same time our ram of the moment, who has been living in tranquil male segregation with his current buddy, an unflappable wether, ever since the previous December, begins to attack fence posts and beat up the trees in his paddock, battering his thick frontal bone against their trunks until the bark is scarred and his horns bloody at the base. Even a human can smell his rank, acrid scent from fifty yards away, and the ewes, with their more sophisticated nasal receptors, can pick it up across several fields. He is stating, without the smallest possibility of misunderstanding, that he would like to join his harem – *right now* – but my usual reaction is, Not so fast, my lad! For from my point of view, the date on which he goes in to the ewes must be carefully considered, since it will influence much of the coming year.

The traditional rule-of-thumb timespan for ovine gestation is between Guy Fawkes Day and April Fools' Day – November 5th to April lst. If you want early lambs for showing purposes, or to catch the Easter market, and are prepared to risk a late cold snap next spring, you might put the ram in earlier – say September; equally, if you plan a skiing holiday at Easter, you could delay the arrival of lambs by putting the ram in with his ewes in mid-November.

Keeping him waiting, however, is fraught with anxiety because he is strong and single-minded. Once a fence-post snaps off under his onslaughts, he will be over the wire like a hurdler, and as soon as the ewes scent his proximity, they will crowd up to the nearest point of their own fence, egging on his advances.

So my calculations have to be quickly made. In this sheltered valley, the spring grass usually starts growing in mid-March. If the ewes are served in mid-October, lambs can be expected from the end of the first week in March onward – that, at least, is the theory. In practice, this timetable can easily be thrown out by bad weather – late frosts and snow that hold back the grass – or by the ewes' own metabolisms. If they are too fat or too thin at the time of tupping, they will not conceive on their first cycle, so you end up with lambs born over a period of weeks rather than days.

This is tiresome, because the efficient management of sheep requires all medical treatment to be performed en bloc. Lambs have to be vaccinated against the most deadly clostridial diseases, as well as tagged and dosed for worms, and it is far easier to do them all at the same time. If there is a wide variation in age and weight it not only makes calculating dosage more tricky, but it is all too easy to omit one of these routine procedures because the lamb was out of sync with the rest of his generation, should have been dealt with separately, but wasn't.

Shepherds with large flocks use hormone-impregnated sponges to induce all their ewes to ovulate at the same time, and often back these up with a 'teaser' – a vasectomised ram – to get the ladies in the right frame of mind when the approved sire is introduced, but these sophisticated methods are not for a holding as small as ours, where Nature allied to a vigorous young ram can be relied on to do the business without recourse to veterinary science.

Nor do we scan the pregnant ewes to discover how many lambs each is carrying. Again, this can save a large flockmaster a lot in feeding-costs, because by separating ewes expecting singles from those carrying twins or triplets, and feeding them proportionately less concentrates in the vital six weeks before lambing, the nutrition goes where it is needed most.

So the date for tupping is decided upon, and the next important step is to pen the ram, trim his feet, inspect his teeth, and generally check him over. Though our experience with Agamemnon had taught us the folly of making a pet of a ram, we discovered during the four-year reigns of each of his successors that a wild, scared ram is even more of a menace, and it is well worth spending some time taming and handling any promising candidate for stud duties while he is still young enough to control with relative ease.

It is essential to be able to put on a halter or head-collar, for example, and teach him to stand quietly while tied to an upright. It is also worthwhile making sure that the post is a strong one. Weeks of works are cancelled out the moment he finds he can pull free from whatever is restraining him, or lift up the hurdles of his pen with a crafty twist of the horns, because once he knows it is possible, he will try to do it again. And again.

The same applies to the ewes, and it is interesting to see the wide variety in their responses to being caught up and handled. They may all look alike, but temperamentally each has her own quirks and eccentricities. Some will let you pick up their front hoofs without demur, but kick furiously the moment you lift a hind leg. When this happens, the only hope is to take a good grip, pin her against the side of the pen with your knee, and hang on grimly while she rears up, lies down, and tries to batter your hand to a pulp. It helps to remember that she will eventually stop struggling, though sometimes it seems to take a very long time before she accepts the situation. By then, foot-shears, sponge, and antibiotic spray will have been sent flying, and you must retain your grip on the leg to be treated while cautiously retrieving them and getting to work on the overgrown horn.

Unless sheep spend a proportion of each day on a hard surface like concrete, their hoofs grow surprisingly fast and often very unevenly, with most lameness resulting from dirt or gravel working into the gap that develops between overgrown horn and the quick.

All sheep are quick to learn to follow a bucket of feed, and my rule is never to try to cheat with an empty bucket, for a small flock is so much more easily led than driven. But before picking up the lure to bring the flock into the farmyard, I make sure that the gates are already open, the pens in position, and long troughs prepared to receive the contents of the bucket, because any form of hold-up may provoke some suspicious old ewe at the back to conclude that you mean mischief.

This is when the expensive handling gear – sheeted hurdles, guillotine gate and so on – that I bought way back when we acquired our first ewes, really comes into its own. Sorting out the culls who must be sent to market, from the ewes for breeding, has to be done objectively, with no room for sentimentality over dear old favourites who are past their prime, and you need to examine each separately. Gates, hurdles, and swing doors all slot together, and building the most convenient layout with the available equipment is as enjoyable as playing with outsize Meccano.

I usually construct a narrow race that accommodates three ewes at once, with the guillotine at one end. This is raised and lowered by a rope and pulley, so one can drive the sheep from behind and let it down as soon as three are in position. At the other end of the race is a sliding gate, so animals can be let through singly into a smaller pen, and this in turn gives onto another sliding gate attached to the drafting barrier, which swings to and fro to direct breeding ewes and culls into separate enclosures.

There is a separate triangular pen for treating any sheep that needs it, and this has an adjustable neck-clamp gate to hold her still while the solo handler is busy reading ear-tags, checking udders (very important), and grappling with fiddly syringes, needles and marker sprays which have an infuriating habit of dropping into any available mud. Only when every breeding ewe candidate has been identified, examined, wormed, and foot-trimmed can she be considered ready for the impatient ram.

After so many months of idleness, he will probably be on the fat side, but no sooner has he entered the ewes' field and caught their fascinating scent than he will go into overdrive. No need to tell him to *stiffen the sinews, summon up the blood*: with his head thrown back and nostrils flaring, he looks like a representation of Lust from a medieval Book of Hours.

The excited ewes then crowd together and he disappears into the midst of them. There follows a lot of skipping and chasing, shoving, and mock charges until he sorts out who is and who is not ready for his attentions, and at this point I stroll away and leave him to it.

Three weeks later he will have slimmed down dramatically. If he still cosies up to one particular ewe or another, you can be fairly sure he has not finished his business, but by the end of a month he will probably lie a little apart from his harem, and will not mind returning to the bachelor life once more.

The next three months are a peaceful period for the shepherd. Provided they were in good condition when tupped, the ewes will do well on grass alone until Christmas, and only if hard weather cracks in after New Year's Day will you need to add hay and a little flaked maize and oats to their rations, taking care not to overdo the extra feed, because a fluctuating level of nutrition – either too much or too little – may cause a pregnant ewe to develop the horrible condition of pregnancy toxaemia, when the lambs growing inside her make over-heavy demands on her body reserves, so that her own fat breaks down into toxins, in effect poisoning her.

What you are aiming at is a steady level of condition during this stage of gestation, with the ewes neither starving nor bloated, and this depends a good deal on the weather and how much grass is available. Hungry ewes are not slow to make their wishes clear, but once you start putting out even the smallest amount of extra feed daily, you have to continue or face a barrage of complaint every time you are spotted carrying a bucket. Some eyes are always on the watch, and when you have no vast acreage in which to disappear, whichever ewe is currently playing spotter in the flock will quickly alert her mates to your presence. Since continuous bleating at close quarters is extraordinarily wearing, it is worth being sure the extra grub is really needed before beginning to dole it out.

These early to mid stages of pregnancy are an agreeable, undemanding interlude when I find myself leaning on gates a good deal, idly watching from a distance as the expectant ladies alternate their routine perambulations with little lie-downs in favoured spots – against a sunny bank, perhaps, or with their spreading backs propped against the trunks of trees – but all too soon the final six weeks before lambing are on us, and there is work to be done.

Any first-lamber must be given two doses of Heptovac P Plus vaccine to protect her against the worst of the ovine clostridial diseases. These are subcutaneous jabs, far more tricky than the straightforward, bang-'em-in-the-bum intramuscular type, and countless times I have shot the dose into my own thumb, or out on the other side of the raised fold of skin, rather than into the layer beneath it, thereby wasting the vaccine, but suffering no ill effect, which is curious when you consider how many deadly diseases are incorporated in that tiny 2ml dose. The jabs for first-time mothers are meant to be administered a month apart, with the second one a fortnight before lambing. At the same time the old-stagers will need a booster jab to reactivate their immunity and pass it on to their lambs. Since the vaccine doesn't keep for more than two months, you ought to work backwards from the expected first lambing date, six weeks for the first-time mothers, then a month's interval, and finally, a fortnight before lambing for all the pregnant ewes.

It sounds simple enough, but even so I have often let the first date slip past me without remembering it, thus bringing the two jabs closer together than the recommended interval. Fortunately this seems to make no difference to their effectiveness.

Up to this time, the unborn lambs have been hardly growing – not with the embryonic diapause of bears and badgers, for sheep are superficial central implanters – but nevertheless Nature has programmed them to use a similar strategy, in order to ensure that their offspring are born in the most favourable possible conditions as the weather grows warmer and food is plentiful. Six weeks before lambing, however, the foetuses begin to grow rapidly, and this is when the ewes need high protein cubes to boost their body reserves, though again you have to be careful not to overdo it: starting with a mere half-pound of cubes apiece, and gradually working up to three or four pounds per head per day, divided into two meals to prevent acidosis.

Then there is such shoving and pushing, such scrimmaging and butting round the troughs as they use shoulders and horns to secure a decent helping, that an agile dog could run along the line of broad backs without disturbing them. To avoid being trampled or biffed about I take care to dole out the feed from the other side of the fence. A couple of minutes, and it is all gone; the last cubes chased into the corners and greedily licked out, while some knowing old ladies go to the length of turning the troughs upside down in case the odd escapee has rolled underneath. *Waste not, want not,* is the motto as the ewes meander away to settle down for another long, refreshing nap.

As their waistlines expand to truly frightening proportions, dozing takes up more and more of the day, and you begin to worry that they are going to collapse as they lumber about the field. Twice, indeed, I have known ewes so heavily burdened that for the last ten days they were unable to stand up at all. One eventually gave birth to live triplets, and recovered the use of her legs; the other had two dead and one live lamb, but had become so lopsided that she could not stand to suckle him. On the other hand, a lively two-year-old ewe whom I thought had a week to go, surprised us by emerging from the shelter of a hedge one frosty March morning , trailing what looked like a white wave at her heels.

'What's she got – twins?' I asked, as Duff drew back the curtains and picked up the binoculars we keep on the windowsill.

'Two, three, four... Good lord, it's a whole platoon!' he said in disbelief, 'and they all look fine.'

That ewe brought them all up, too, with only minimal help from me in the form of extra rations and lamb pellets as soon as they were old enough to nibble them, and family discipline was exemplary. Instead of wandering off on their own or larking about with their contemporaries, all her lambs stuck close together, and the faintest bleat brought the whole bunch rushing to her side, desperate not to miss a chance to suckle. Though she looked perfectly well and never went 'poor,' I think the strain on her constitution must have been considerable, because for the rest of her breeding life she only produced one lamb at a time.

Twins are the norm, which is lucky because from every point of view two is the most satisfactory number for a ewe to rear. A teat apiece, so less opportunity for one side to go unused; no queuing at the milk bar, as the weakest of a set of triplets is obliged to; and no over-fat single to outstrip his fellows in development and reach sexual maturity before the rest.

But this is getting ahead of myself. The next and most dramatic landmark in the whole shepherding cycle is the arrival of the lambs themselves. This involves a certain amount of stage management, reconfiguring the barns and sheds for maximum convenience and security. The first step is to collect all available interlocking hurdles, some of which will have been used for other purposes since last year's lambing, and may be found moonlighting as barriers to stop ram lambs butting the horsebox, for example, blocking a weak place in a hedge, or encircling some hazard such as a cesspit.

When all the hurdles I possess have been recalled to their duty and stacked in the lambing shed, I build half a dozen pens, anchored to 'eyes' set in the wall, and line the lower half of each with paper feed sacks tied to the bars with bindertwine, in order to give each ewe a little world into which her neighbour cannot peer.

Next I seek out the component parts of the Adopter Box – the simple but indispensable aid to fostering spare triplets on to ewes with singles. It is constructed from four sheets of strong plywood with open hooks at each corner into which bars are inserted to hold them in a square. The front sheet has folding doors which close to leave a narrow arch which can be closed round the ewe's neck, leaving her head sticking outside. Side-bars hold her securely in position, able to stand or lie, but quite unable to see behind her, or distinguish whether it is her own lamb or an interloper suckling in the box.

Some ewes accept this arrangement equably, while others throw themselves from side to side as they try to evict the foster lamb, but it is worth persevering with the adoption for four or five days, so both the lambs smell identical, before tentatively allowing the ewe to see her mysteriously augmented family.

This is always an anxious moment, and if she stamps, lowers her head threateningly, or shows any other sign that she has not accepted the foster lamb, one has to step in smartly, push her back into the adopter box, and wait a few more days before trying again. However sticky she may be to begin with, a foster mother makes a very much better job of rearing an orphan than any human can with a bottle or self-feeding unit, not only because she watches out for her offspring all the time instead of once every four hours, but also teaches by example all the life-skills it is going to require.

Once pens and adopter box are strawed down and ready for use, the period of maximum anxiety begins, and to counter it I check over the contents of the lambing bucket. This is rather wider and shallower than a normal bucket, and has a segmented canvas lining with pockets of various shapes and sizes in which to keep all the useful small bits and pieces of equipment I am likely to need: surgical gloves, short and long; lubricant jelly; lambing rope; needles, syringes, and in-date LA broad-spectrum antibiotic, coloured spray, thermometer, scissors, pen and notebook, elastrator and rubber rings, tags and pincers, and so on. Last but not least piece of essential equipment is the Snare, a loop of soft plastic wire that can be threaded behind the ears of an emerging lamb, and soft Lambing Ropes to secure and pull forward its legs.

Compulsively I read and re-read my battered old book about lambing, with its graphic illustrations of every mis-presentation and awkward tangle of legs and heads that the shepherd is ever likely to encounter, plus calm, clear advice on how to correct them.

Despite knowing perfectly well that most ewes give birth unassisted, reading about these potential disasters always makes me cold with apprehension. What if this is the year when everything goes wrong? Lambing is rather like flying a passenger plane: 95% boredom and 5% panic. You watch and wait for hours while nothing happens, then suddenly a great many things happen very quickly, and if you make the wrong decision then, one or more lambs and possibly the ewe may die. The thought comes between me and my sleep, so that ears are constantly on the alert for unusual noises from the sheep-shed for fear of missing those few vital moments.

When action is imminent, however, the signs are clear

enough. First and most reliable is an uncharacteristic reluctance to come to the feeding-trough. Instead of bustling up when she hears the rattle of cubes in the bucket, and digging in among her mates, the ewe in question simply looks after them and turns away like an anorexic teenager disgusted by naked greed. This is your moment to separate her from the rest of the flock and gently drive her into a prepared pen.

She may settle down at once with a sigh of relief, which probably means the birth is still several hours away; or she may go round and round the pen, digging up the bedding, glancing at her sides, lying down, getting up again and showing similar signs of restlessness. This is when it is useful to have the pen partially screened, because while testing its boundaries, she may take a fancy to the lamb in the next-door pen – an interest its mother is likely to resent, and the last thing you want is two embattled ewes butting one another through the bars.

Constant supervision is not necessary at this stage of proceedings, and may even be counter-productive. I often think that ewes prefer to see as little of humans as possible while engaged in the very private process of giving birth, and deliberately time delivery to coincide with dawn. A couple of quick checks on progress at 11pm and 5am keeps the single-handed shepherd up to speed without too much night-time disturbance, and it is a joyful bonus if the dawn check reveals a couple of fluffy newcomers in the pen.

If things are going wrong, however, decision-time looms, and this is where a head-torch becomes invaluable. The lamb should be positioned like a diver, with the forefeet just in advance of its nose, but unless you have a good light it is surprisingly difficult to be sure exactly what is emerging once the dark, balloon-like waterbag has ruptured. The head is easy to recognise, but is there one tiny hoof or two just under the chin? And are those hoofs the right way round? Do they, in fact, belong with that particular head?

There is only one way to find out. On with gloves, slather them with jelly, and carefully work your fingers past the head, on down the neck and sharply angled shoulder-bone to the leg, making sure they are connected all the way, first on one side and then the other. If one leg is bent back, you must push the head into the uterus again, locate the bent leg and bring it forward and then, if the lamb still refuses to budge, pull the loop of cord through the handle of the Y-shaped 'lambing instrument,' and fit it behind the lamb's ears, wedging its chin and hoofs into the angle at the top of the handle. Then, keeping a good grip on the loose end of cord at the bottom of the handle, pull steadily towards the ewe's back feet, and the lamb should emerge as naturally as possible. Quickly clear the nose and mouth from the enveloping membrane and, as soon as it takes a breath, put it right by the ewe's head so that she can lick it dry.

If the lamb is floppy and doesn't breathe immediately, urgent resuscitation actions include tickling its nostrils with a straw, pouring cold water into its ear or, if this fails, picking it up by the hind legs and swinging it vigorously to and fro can kickstart it into life. There is usually a pause of twenty minutes or so before the birth of the next lamb, and during this time the ewe will be very busy cleaning up her firstborn, encouraging it to get up and suckle, and talking to it non-stop in a whole range of pianissimo grunts and bleats before a new series of contractions turn her thoughts inward again.

Birth is a strenuous business, and it is always a marvel to me how a ewe can produce three or even four lambs in a small pen without trampling or over-lying any of them. Somehow she manages to avoid damaging these fragile newborns, (who must be more resilient than they look) and any notion of giving the family more room to manoeuvre must be firmly resisted. The closer they are during the first hours of life, the better they will bond, for if even a few feet separate the ewe from her lamb, she will suspect it belongs elsewhere and may even attack it.

Another common mis-presentation which needs speedy assistance is when, as expected, you see two hoofs appear, but instead of a nose they are accompanied a small white tail. More careful inspection reveals that the lamb is the wrong way round, and the best thing to do is grip tail and both hind legs firmly, and draw out the lamb in one swift horizontal movement – swift, because if you delay it will suffocate as soon as the umbilical cord is ruptured.

Both leg-back and posterior presentation are easy enough for a relatively inexpert shepherd to manage – keep calm, think it out, use a head-torch, gloves, and plenty of lubricating jelly – but when it comes to anything really challenging like a breech presentation, for example, or a tangle of limbs and heads which are hard to identify, I find the best thing is to recognise my limitations and call the vet. An expensive option, but one always learns something from watching the pro sort out a problem which, minutes earlier, might have seemed beyond resolution. Over-all the saving in life justifies the call-out fee.

All these possible hazards make lambing sound more difficult than it really is because, as I said, most ewes cope fine on their own. They are also far better than any human at knowing what their lambs need in the way of food and shelter. Cuddled up against mum's back or flank, extremes of temperature, rain, or wind scarcely trouble them at all, and though I like to have the capacity to bring the whole flock under cover when the weather is really severe, I leave the door open for them to go in and out when they want to.

Triplets are a problem. Leave them for the ewe to rear on her own and more than likely one will slowly starve, or end up a miserable skinny travesty of a lamb by weaning time. Rear one artificially, and you are condemning yourself to six weeks of tricky, time-consuming measuring, mixing, and administering formula milk, the constant danger of upsetting the lamb's digestion or letting it get chilled, and even if it survives these hazards you are still likely to end up with a weanling that is fat and thin in all the wrong places, pot-bellied yet scraggy-necked, and scarcely a credit to the flock. It will also be far too tame, and bleat heart-rendingly whenever it sees you. By the time it is weaned, it will have cost most of what you expect to sell it for in powdered milk, emergency medicaments, and lamb pellets – and that is not factoring in the time and anxiety you will have expended in its care.

Though it makes much the best economic sense, it is psychologically extremely difficult for the shepherd to remove the third lamb immediately after birth and knock it on the head. Looking at the third arrival curled up in the straw, or wobbling with splayed legs as it nuzzles blindly for a teat, you forget all about the time and trouble it will cause and long to give it a fighting chance. This is where the Adopter Box is such a blessing, and why it is worth making every effort to persuade any mother-of-one to accept a second son or daughter.

All too often, however, there is no suitable candidate to act as foster-mother and, faced with the stark choice between bottle-feeding or euthanasia, you opt for the former.

The received wisdom is that if you do decide to hand-rear the surplus lamb, you should take away either the biggest or the smallest, the thinking behind this being that the biggest is most likely to adapt to and survive this unnatural method of getting its grub, while the smallest is the least loss if it fails to make the transition from mum's to powdered milk, and the remaining pair will do better if they are evenly matched.

Should all three lambs be much of a muchness in size, they may all succeed in getting a fair share of the available milk if left with their mother but the strain of rearing three will take a heavy toll on her, and she will need supplementary rations. This, in turn, means keeping the family separate from the rest of the flock, since the other ewes will otherwise leave their own lambs and swoop on the extra food like a flock of vultures, and there will be much bleating and kerfuffle and chance of mismothering before all the families are matched up once more.

Ewes are absolutely ruthless about butting away strange lambs who make the innocent mistake of trying to suckle from the wrong udder. It is one of the main difficulties when trying to arrange adoptions. You'd think that a ewe which had lost one of her twins and was bursting with milk would be glad of an orphaned replacement to relieve the pressure – but no, she will try every trick in the book to deny any lamb but her own the use of her second teat. She will kick, butt, and hold back her milk, her struggles so intimidating the interloper that unless the ewe is strictly confined and unable to see or smell him, he will either starve or be battered to death.

All this flashes through your mind as you try to decide how to handle the question of triplets, but it is one to which I have never settled on the most satisfactory answer

So lambing and its aftermath looms large in the shepherding calendar as a fraught period, full of known and unknown hazards, and so it has always been. Two thousand years ago, Jesus was describing an age-old scenario with His parable of the one lost sheep who gave the shepherd more trouble than all the other ninety-nine in the flock, but also more joy when it finally turned up safe and sound.

Seeing a bottle-reared or adopted lamb racing about the field with the rest of its generation after a rocky start is immensely satisfying, but they do tend to be unusually accident-prone. They fall into ditches or wander into ponds. They get caught in brambles, or thread their heads through squared wire fences, pull back in panic, and break their necks. It's not really that they have a death-wish: they just ain't been brought up proper. Though ewes sometimes appear to be idle, greedy, downright negligent mums, their vigilance is none the less for being understated, and when they see their offspring in danger, they take positive action.

This was brought home to me one foggy morning in late March, when from the gate of our biggest field you could hardly see across to the far fence. As Duff set out for a walk with the labrador, he heard barking from the direction of the village, but took no notice. When I went to lead the horses out about twenty minutes later, however, I was horrified to find our younger alpaca wallowing in the trough by the gate, bleeding into the water. Two ewes were upside down nearby, their legs and bellies ripped, and another had her head buried in a hedge, with a large chunk missing from her hindquarters.

As the mist swirled apart, I saw a blur of movement two hundred yards away by the far fence, where a rangy sheepdog-type had the rest of the ewes pinned in a tight bunch against the wire. It was running in a semi-circle, yapping continuously, while the sheep stamped their forefeet and surged back and forth, trying to escape. Farther away up the hill lay a fat, grey-muzzled labrador with heaving sides, which had evidently run itself to a standstill.

I felt such a surge of fury that it took my own breath away. Hastily loosing the horses into the adjoining field, I lifted and heaved the alpaca out of the bloody water, then ran towards the circling dog, but when I grabbed it by the scruff the little brute snapped at me, wrenched free and took off in the direction of the village. The labrador was wearing no collar, so I tied the horses' rope round its neck and tried to lead it, but it was so exhausted it was more a question of dragging it along the ground as far as our kennel. I bolted the door, then shouted to Duff, who had just reappeared, to call the vet and the police and ran back to the field.

The mist was lifting, and the paddock looked like a battlefield. Three injured ewes were in a bad way, and so was the alpaca. The ram was unscathed, but his companion wether's intestines were dangling round his hocks. All were too shocked to move.

And where were the lambs? Though the ewes who had been pinned against the fence were bleating urgently, there wasn't a sign of them.

The vet arrived in double-quick time, and the police very soon after. Duff took charge of the hunt for the attackers, but they weren't hard to identify because everyone from the postman to the publican knew who owned them. Sure enough, they were back in his garden, the open gate showing how they had escaped.

The vet and I carried and drove the walking wounded into the sheepshed, and it wasn't until after he had treated the worst of their injuries, administered antibiotics and euthanased the poor wether, that I had time to search for the missing lambs.

Half a dozen were huddled in a narrow, thorny gap between the hedge and the wire fence, four more cowering behind a field shelter, and the rest lying low under the lip of a bank. Despite their own terror when the dogs attacked, the ewes must have ordered their offspring to scatter and hide, and so effective had that command been that the lambs had stayed in hiding ever since. They were all present, and miraculously quite uninjured.

The owner of the dogs had been at work at the time of the attack, and was surprised and indignant that in his absence some hand unknown had released them from his garden. When convinced that they were responsible, however, he had the ringleader put down, and sent the old labrador to live with his ex-wife in a town, to prevent a repeat performance. He also paid most of the vet's bills.

It took four months of daily treatment to heal the big open wounds of the worst-affected ewes, but eventually they did scab over, leaving only dents to show where chunks had been bitten from their bellies and haunches and remind us that though we may regard them as harmless family pets, where sheep are concerned, all dogs are potential killers.

Watching the antics of young lambs towards sunset on

a frosty spring evening is one of my great pleasures. Skipping and cavorting, twisting their little bodies into improbable contortions and making spasmodic high jumps onto walls and banks, they race back and forth in packs. Two or three will start a game of follow-my-leader and, seeing them flash past, others join in until you have twelve or fifteen lambs tearing about in the gloaming. They look quite crazy, but this mad outburst of energy is really just a sensible way of preparing for a cold night. Thoroughly warmed by the exercise, they can maintain their body temperature however low the thermometer drops, each with its mother's warm bulk as a bulwark against the most cutting wind.

It is partly as protection against the elements that I leave my ewes' tails as Nature intended. Within the triangular shelter formed by hind legs and a long tail, the udder is less likely to get chapped and sore, and the lambs have a cosy place in which to suckle.

All too soon, though, the frenetic evening frolicking gives way to adult gravity, as the youngsters copy their mothers and buckle down to the serious business of filling their bellies with as much grass as they can, while remaining on the alert for the smallest sign that mum is ready to feed them again. Sometimes they misinterpret her signal, and dash over to her only to be rebuffed as she refuses to stand for them. Her need for them is always directly related to the state of her udder, and the vigorous pummelling it receives from the half-grown lambs as an incentive to let down her milk makes one wonder why she puts up with them at all.

As the summer months pass, the bond between mother and offspring weakens progressively, and gender differences become more marked. Gone are the adorable, vulnerable, animated cottonwool balls. The ewe lambs form gangs, like teenage girls, while the young rams lambs go through an 'awkward age' at about twenty weeks. Leggy and gawky, with heads that look too big for their bodies, they also become unattractively aggressive, butting and mounting one another – teenage yobs, in fact – so addicted to fighting that their prominent horns are often decorated with blood.

This is the moment, before they can turn their testosterone-fuelled attention to their mothers and sisters, that one must grasp the nettle and separate the sexes by as far as the available territory allows. I find that two strong fences, with a field in-between, is the minimum needed to prevent the young gentlemen from forcing their way back to their mums in the first forty-eight hours of separation, for at this stage they are not only splendid jumpers but also very stoical about shoving through strands of barbed wire, leaving strips of skin behind, and once they have discovered a way to get through the barriers, they will do it again and again.

The ideal solution is to remove them from earshot by lodging them temporarily with family or friends who could do with a posse of mobile lawnmowers. As soon as they settle in their new quarters with no females to compete for, the young rams grow and put on weight surprisingly quickly, and before long another decision looms: is any one of them outstanding enough to sell as a breeding prospect?

So many males are born each year that only the exceptional animal makes the grade as a stud ram. Looks and pedigree are important in pure-bred animals, but they are not the only requirements; it is not easy to describe, but gradually every shepherd comes to recognise the particular proud carriage and eye-catching quality of a real star, which goes far beyond the usual breed descriptions of desirable attributes such as *Ears: inclined to be long and broad; chest: deep, with well-filled brisket;* and *underline: good, straight, naked;* not to mention the all-important testicles. I shall never forget the time I was so carried away by the beauty of a young ram that I forgot to check these and bought a stud with a single ball. It worked perfectly well, but I am sure the seller burst out laughing the moment I drove away with it.

So if the answer to the breeding-prospect question is No – and it usually is – the ram lambs' future resolves itself quickly and brutally into two options: market or local abattoir? Personally I prefer the latter. Though it is never agreeable to hustle your home-bred stock down the ramp of the trailer and into the slaughter-house lairage to await their fate, at least you know that the waiting will not be long and exactly what that fate will be. The ram lambs have been given a good, natural life for five or six months. They will die with the least stress possible and, if you find their death distressing, you should not be in the business of rearing livestock.

No such certainty can be expected if you decide to take your lambs to market. For a start, you don't know who will buy them: whether they will be run on and fattened for a few more months, or crammed in a lorry and driven hundreds of miles, possibly even exported, before ending up at some foreign abattoir whose standards might be very different from our own.

It is mid-August by the time we take our ram lambs to slaughter. Since late Spring the ewes will have been shedding their fleeces, looking ragged and unkempt during May and June, when you can often see them lying comfortably sprawled at siesta time with corvids industriously plucking out loose tufts of the kemp for purposes of their own. By July, however, the last of the old fleece has gone, replaced by a sleek, short coat more elegantly smooth than any shearer could achieve.

Since man-made fabrics have largely replaced wool in the modern economy, it now costs more to pay a shearer than you can hope to recover in the sale of wool, so naturally – shed fleeces are a bonus. It takes three or four generations to transfer the shedding gene from the Wiltshire Horn to woolly sheep, but even then you are apt to breed animals with long tufts of semi-wool along their backs, getting the worst of both worlds, which is why, despite the drawback of the horns, we stick doggedly to pure-bred Wilts.

After the departure of the boisterous, aggressive boys, the female side of the flock can be left together for another month before the ewe lambs are weaned. They will not have depended on their mothers' milk for some time, but all the same the parting has to be handled carefully. Again, if you can get ewes and lambs out of earshot of one another the trauma is diminished not only for them but also for humans who want to sleep through the night, but after being separated from their lambs, the ewes must be allowed only minimal grazing for a week at least while you keep a sharp eye on the state of their udders.

Mastitis can strike with terrible speed, and you have to move fast to counter it. Immediate milking of the affected teat plus long-acting antibiotics usually saves the ewe, though it leaves her unable to rear twins, but you have to act at once. If, while looking round the stock one evening, you happen to notice an animal walking stiffly with her hind legs far apart, or lying on her own in the corner of a field shelter, it's no good thinking, *I'll get her in and take a look in the morning,* because by morning she may well be dead.

Sheep are social animals who seek safety in numbers, and one lying on her own is always a danger signal. The process of drying-off their remaining milk supply always seems to take an age, but by degrees their udders become paler and slacker until by October they have almost vanished, and it is time to put them on better pasture to build up their fat reserves before the year comes full circle and it is tupping time again.

October is the prime month for sheep sales up and down the country. The Breed Society sales for pedigree animals are often preceded by showing classes for lambs, shearlings, and older stock of both sexes, with the best animals available on display, washed to snowy whiteness, horns polished, hoofs properly trimmed. Most of them are halter-broken up to a point, and it is instructive to see the judge's assessment as he arranges the contestants in order of merit.

Prices can go ridiculously high as rival bidders compete for the prizewinners, but though it is always interesting to meet other breeders and hear the sheep world's gossip, since we deal in small numbers and seldom have more than ten or a dozen ewe lambs for sale, I prefer to advertise them on the Wiltshire Horn Society's website and sell them privately. Only by talking directly to a prospective buyer can you get an idea of what sort of home your stock will be going to, and I always take the precaution of asking how much grazing is available to him or her. In October when the grass is long and lush, many smallholders forget what it will look like in February, and miscalculate the numbers they can over-winter without running short of grub.

It is fascinating to see the different approaches taken by private buyers. Some arrive with a trailer, cast a quick look over the sheep, agree to your price and drive away within an hour. Others start trying to haggle before they even take a look at what they have come to buy. Some stand well away from the pen and show no desire to handle the sheep. Others check every one for teeth, teats, hoofs and condition, marking the ones they want.

'I suppose these are all your rejects,' said one lofty lady, looking contemptuously at six of my very best shearlings. 'Well, I don't like *that* one – or *that* one for a start. They're not what I'm looking for at all. What else have you got for sale?'

Grinding my teeth, I showed her my ewe lambs, who were still out in the field, and asked if she wanted me to bring them in so that she could take a close look at them.

'No, but I'd like to see their breeding,' she said. 'Are they all registered?'

Over a cup of tea, I showed her the paperwork. She kept trying to denigrate my shearlings and to beat me down on the price, but I was beginning to dislike her manner and refused to budge. Both Duff and I were relieved when she drove away without buying anything, and congratulated ourselves on keeping our tempers.

Later that evening, the telephone rang. 'Barbara here,' said the lofty voice. 'Just ringing to tell you I'll buy the lot at your price. The shearlings and the lambs as well. I'd like you to bring them over to me next Monday in your trailer.'

I hesitated, half wanting to tell her to jump in the lake, half knowing that it would be stupid to turn down a perfectly good offer. Besides, I was curious to know what kind of set-up she had.

As the silence lengthened, she said impatiently, 'What's the matter? Can't you do that?'

'Well, it's a good fifty miles each way – '

'Don't worry. I'll pay for the petrol.'

Oh, you will indeed, I thought. You certainly will.

Luckily, such buyers are rare. Much more often I find myself selling to a variety of sheep-fanciers ranging from the young couple who have spent their all on a house with five or six acres and want to start a flock for the smallest outlay possible, to the ageing empty-nesters where the wife hankers after animals on whom to lavish love and attention, and the husband is looking for an outdoor hobby to liven up his retirement.

There's no haggling over price in the second case. Buyers are keen, the cheque-book poised, yet even at the risk of losing a sale, the vendor's conscience won't be easy unless a few tactful enquiries are made, and all too often a few minutes' conversation reveals a hidden snag. Arthritis. Emphysema. A dodgy back or a hip in need of replacement. A field half a mile from their house. Yes, it is thick with grass now, but it won't be by February, and they may find that carrying hay is more than they can cope with. Hungry ewes can be quite rough when competing for their concentrates, and anyone not too steady on his pins may be knocked over in the rush. Have they got anyone – er – younger who could lend a hand?

I find it a relief when these private sales are over and done with and the money banked. Selling in the nearest livestock market is very much simpler, and this is where we take our culls; for the last, rather melancholy task of my shepherding year is to get in the ewes, get out the lambing record, and make a hard-headed decision on which to retain for breeding, and which to send for slaughter. After two months' steady grazing, free from the cares of motherhood, their teats will have shrunk almost to invisibility and any hollows in their flanks filled out until they look plump and jolly, well able to cope with another set of lambs, but the record book may tell a different tale.

The first consideration is age. Years of surrendering to the impulse to keep some elderly favourite for just one more season has finally convinced me that breeding from old ewes is a mug's game, because it is bound to be the one winter when everything goes wrong. A long and bitter freeze-up in January. Continuous deluges in February which turn the pasture into mud soup. Cutting winds straight from Siberia in March. While the younger ewes adapt easily enough, the dear old lady may begin to struggle. She will need extra food, and that means arranging special, solitary meals, shutting her in a pen while her mates circle like the troops of Midian, then remembering to come back to let her out rather than waking with a jolt at 2am, realising she is still confined.

And even if she lambs without difficulty and presents you with healthy twins, she may not have the bodily resources to produce enough milk for them both, which lands you with a whole other set of problems.

No: even among sheep, child-bearing is a job for the young and strong. Some breeds last longer than others – I have a photograph of a Welsh Mountain ewe aged 23 with her latest set of twins – but in general I think it sensible to call time no later than eight years of age.

So out go the oldest ewes, making room for the shearlings

I have retained, and after checking for physical defects such as deformed feet or the residual lumpiness of mastitis, I get out the stained and scribbled-over log book in which I noted down lambing events as they happened, I check for those who gave the most and the least trouble last spring. Who needed assistance or medication. Who tried to toss one of her twins out of the pen and had to be restrained in the Adopter Box; who refused to let her lambs suckle.

It is only six months since all these dramas were at the forefront of my mind, but it is amazing how quickly you forget them once the peaceful routine of summer becomes established. By the time I fill in my official record book and send off forms to register the new lambs in early autumn, the bald statements of breeding, ear-tag numbers, sexes and dates of birth give little idea of the highs and lows, triumphs and disasters which followed each other in swift succession during the fraught fortnight of lambing and this may, in itself, be a mercy.

If I knew precisely the annual cost in physical and emotional energy that keeping a small flock would entail, let alone the expenditure in time and money, would I forego the pleasure of watching ewes and lambs scattered across the green fields on summer evenings, and opt instead for gang-mowers to keep the pasture tidy? I don't think so, but it might be a close-run thing.

It was only when I learned to spin and Duff commissioned a beautiful new spinning-wheel from a master-craftsman of the Somerset Guild, for a Christmas present, that my Wiltshire Horns' lack of wool began to seem less of a plus than a problem. Though clumps of the crinkly kemp that covered them could easily be gathered from the fences in Spring, with the best will in the world you couldn't spin it. The staples were too short and coarse to card: it was far more suitable for lining the nests of birds, who did indeed make the most of it. For a few months I bought or begged small quantities of sheep's wool from friends and relations, but a whole fleece was more than I could cope with, and these odd bits and pieces tended to be ones that wouldn't make the grade for the wool marketing board.

Imagine my delight, then, when for my next birthday Duff presented me with three young alpacas – Shadrach, Meshak, and Abed-Nego – whose dams had been imported by air from Chile when long-standing restrictions on bringing livestock from South America were relaxed in the 1980s.

For a spinner, alpaca fleece is the *creme de la creme*, its long, soft, silky staple has exactly the right texture to retain a twist; gossamer-light, because every strand is hollow, and very clean since it contains no lanolin. There is, moreover, just enough crimp or crinkle in each strand to prevent it slipping through the spinner's fingers, and instead of being limited to a choice between boring white or black, alpacas come in a whole palette of colours: apricot, chocolate, grey, ivory shading to pink, ginger, and russet as well as black and the purest snowflake white. Blend two or more of these, and you have an unlimited number of combinations: black, ginger and grey, for instance; or apricot, ivory and chocolate. For a spinner such variety opens the way to a undreamed of possibilities. Very excited, we drove over to Sussex to collect the animals.

The long approach lane to the alpaca farm was lined with well-spaced trees, and flanked on each side by close-nibbled paddocks fenced with high-tensile wire. As we wove slowly over the potholes, I had plenty of time to stare at the dozens – possibly hundreds – of grazing alpacas of all sizes, colours, and gradations of fleece from huge, unshorn teddy-bears to slender, elegant creatures that might have looked like deer if their little heads had not been topped with frivolous fluffy tufts, like Ascot hats.

Young and old, large and small, they padded abstractedly over the turf with the graceful gliding movement of animals whose front and hind legs move laterally, like camels, exuding such a sense of exotic serenity that we were instantly captivated.

But how to choose two from such an *embarras de richesse?*

'Here are the young geldings,' said Terry, the rangy Australian showing us round as he opened a gate. 'No use for stud now, but there's nothing wrong with their fleeces.'

These were what we wanted. After a shocked look at the price list for females, I had no wish to breed alpacas, but the geldings were a more reasonable £500 apiece; quite enough to pay for materials to keep a spinning-wheel busy.

Curious eyes followed us as we moved through the bunch of two-year-old males, their long necks undulating, and a persistent high-pitched humming vibrating through their ranks.

'That's the noise they make when they're just kinda worried,' said our guide. 'If they're frightened, it's more like a bark. Now, which do you like the look of?'

Of course, I liked them all, but one in particular had caught my eye. Most of his coat was a clear blue-grey, but black legs and a shaggy black cap with a white fringe distinguished him from his mates. His face and throat were also white, and his neck seemed extra long since it rose abruptly from his back, almost at a right-angle instead of a gentle curve.

'That one,' I said, pointing, but for some reason our guide took no notice, urging us to look at the others and feel the luxuriance of their fleeces before deciding.

Since we were complete newcomers to the world of alpacas, I thought we had better follow expert guidance, and before long we had chosen a fine, tall, ivory-fleeced gelding with a long aristocratic face, and a delicately-boned chocolate overlaid with russet. These allowed themselves to be separated from the rest with very little fuss. Together we had begun to herd them through a series of gates to where we had left our trailer when, seeing me glancing back yet again at the grey-and-white alpaca, Terry stopped abruptly.

'You really fancy that little fella, don't you?' he said.

'Well, yes...'

He nodded. 'I could tell you did, but the trouble is, we can't sell him 'cos he's got dropped fetlocks, see. Never straightened out after he was unpacked.'

'*Unpacked?*' It conjured up an image of a yummy mummy with a Louis Vuitton suitcase.

'Dropped. Born.' Terry grinned. 'Look at his front feet – they look twice the length of the others, because his pasterns are flat to the ground, but they don't bother him any. He gets about just fine. So if you want him for a pet, like, I'll throw him in for free.'

Unerringly, I had fallen for the only deformed animal in the field, but if Terry really was prepared to give him away, who could refuse such an offer?

After a brief lesson on the best way to restrain them (one arm round the base of the neck and the other clasping the body against you) and how to trim the toenails which projected beyond the oval padded feet, plus some advice on jabs against clostridial diseases (our old friend Heptovac-P again) and worms (don't try to drench them: they spit) we drove away in triumph with our trio of alpacas lying good as gold on the floor of the trailer. We all had a lot to learn about one another.

The first surprise, to me, was their indifference to bribery. Every animal I had ever known had a weakness for some kind of titbit, with which one could entice them to approach or follow, but none of the alpacas showed the slightest interest in eating anything but grass, leaves, twigs and bark. Carrots – usually a surefire favourite – were nibbled and discarded; ditto oats, flaked maize, apples, sheepnuts. In stark contrast to sheep and horses, they seemed devoid of ordinary greed.

They were, however, extraordinarily easy to herd. Two

people had only to walk behind with a long rope held between them, and the alpacas would drift peacefully wherever you wanted them to go. It never seemed to occur to them to break back, jump the rope or duck underneath: sometimes it made me think that perhaps they were not very bright. The same suspicion arose when they walked past an open gate time and again, without seizing the opportunity to dash through it and raid the vegetable garden, whereas the sheep would have spotted in a flash the gap in our defences.

Transporting them was a doddle, because they travelled lying down, making a commendably low centre of gravity in the trailer. Better still was the demonstration of what to do if you haven't got a trailer. Pen the alpaca, place a long, medium-weight rope or cord – climbing-rope is perfect – over its loins and tie it in a loose loop. Pick up the alpaca's hind legs one at a time and thread them through the loop, and it will then lie down. A strong man can then pick up the whole animal and put it on the back seat of a car, where it will stay quietly until you undo the loop of rope.

I wouldn't have believed this was possible until I saw it being done, and the alpaca chosen for the demonstration was far from tame. Once tied, it simply accepted the situation and made no move to escape.

When confined to a pen, Shadrach (white), Meshak (brown) and little grey Abed-Nego would start the plaintive high-pitched humming which in alpaca-speak denotes anxiety. They really didn't like being shut in, and I soon realised that although they would tolerate contact with humans, they didn't enjoy it. No chance of having a cosy cuddle with that soft, luxurious fleece. Having reached the age of two without being handled except for the necessary jabs and foot-trimming, they were wary of being touched, and Shadrach in particular would kick energetically when I lifted his hind feet. But the next surprise was to discover how fragile they were physically. Under all the fluff and fleece was an animal much lighter than my big ewes, and nothing like so vigorous a fighter. Kick they might, but their feet did little damage, and so long as the handler refused to let go, very soon they gave up the struggle.

There was a new vocabulary to go with them. Like 95% of the imported alpacas in Britain, mine were Huacayas, pronounced Wuh-kay-as, whose immense fluffy fleeces grow outward to give them a rounded, teddy-bear outline; the remaining 5% belong to a breed called Suris, with long corkscrewing ringlets like those worn by Hassidic Jews, which hang down, floating and rippling as they move. Twenty years ago, when alpacas were new to this country, the males were referred to as Machos, and females as Maidens or Dams, while baby alpacas were Crias. Nowadays there is a tendency to called them simply Boys and Girls, which in my eyes removes some of their exoticism and glamour.

It was yet another surprise to find that despite their usual gentleness and serenity, there would be times when terrible fights would break out among our three alpaca geldings – real knock-down, drag-out affairs when they plainly wanted to hurt one another. It was hard to detect what provoked these ferocious spats. One moment the trio would be grazing peacefully. The next they would be flying about the field with mouths open, making harsh braying screams that sounded like rusty hinges being violently forced open.

'That is certainly the cry of some large carnivore,' said an Indian naturalist who was staying with us, and would not believe it was the alpacas until he saw them with his own eyes.

It was usually Shadrach and Meshak who ganged up on Abed-Nego, but even when chased into a corner he gave as good as he got, and the deformed fetlocks seemed to be no hindrance to his nimbleness. At a standstill, the antagonists would wind their necks together and rear up, then one would seize the other's foreleg and bow down to the ground, apparently trying to bite his opponent's non-existent testicles. Altogether, it was

a most unsettling performance, but it would end as abruptly as it started. After a final bout of spitting copious gobs of green slime at one another, the combatants would turn away, mouths hanging open, and all would be peaceful again.

Some of their personal habits were curious, too. Like antelopes, they seemed to be programmed to deposit dung in the same place, all at the same time, and would make quite a long pilgrimage from one end of the field to the other in order to visit their communal midden. Here the over-nitrogenised grass would grow so thick and rank that no other animal cared to eat it, and the only way to rid the paddock of these unsightly blotches was to strim them close to the ground. They had the sensible habit of urinating backwards, Nature's way of keeping their belly-fleece clean, but a far less sensible – indeed downright dangerous – tendency to cast themselves down in the embers of a bonfire, squirming to and fro in an ecstatic tangle of necks and legs as they worked the ash deep into their coats. A young alpaca boarding with a neighbour singed himself badly in this way, and thereafter we were always careful to ensure that the fire was cold and dead before allowing our boys into any field where we'd had a burn-up.

Summer arrived, and when Shadrach started climbing into the water-trough it was clear that he wanted to off-load his winter woollies. Not that he much enjoyed the process. Shearing alpacas is a specialised job, completely different from shearing sheep, and round here it is generally performed by teams of strong young Antipodeans or South Africans who spend our winter, their summer, shearing at home, and bring their skills to the northern hemisphere between May and August.

We loaded our trio into the trailer and drove to the nearest stud where a team of five were already hard at work catching, shearing, vaccinating, and foot-and-teeth trimming the residents. Instead of sitting them on their haunches like sheep, which would emperil the long fragile necks and legs of alpacas, one brawny shearer would, with a cunning lift-and-twist, cast his client on its side on a carefully-swept square of carpet and, while his mate held down its head, stretch out and shackle fore- and hind legs. With swift, practised strokes, he then shaved away the coarser fibre around neck and legs, before peeling away the fine-textured fleece of the 'blanket' covering back and sides.

A quick flip, and the process was repeated on the alpaca's other side until the whole 'blanket' came free in a beautiful soft springy mass. The shearer's mate, meanwhile, had been scooping up and stuffing all the second-grade fibre into a paper sack and as the *creme de la creme* fell upside down on to the carpet, he would carefully – almost reverently – roll it into a neat bundle and put it into a separate sack.

Let no one suppose for a moment that Shadrach and Co took this treatment meekly. On the contrary, they bellowed their displeasure in an ugly guttural grunting roar known as 'urgling,' which continued nonstop throughout the medical rituals that followed. Toenails were trimmed, teeth levelled with an electric angle-grinder that produced an explosion of white powder, followed by booster jabs for every known disease.

Worst humiliation of all, when the smoothly shorn alpaca, near-naked except for a tuft on the head and tail as protection against flies, was released and returned to his mates, they laid back their ears angrily and spat at him as if he was a complete stranger.

True to form, the English summer turned chilly and windy the week after the alpacas lost their fluffy, insulating coats, and I worried that they might catch cold. Since their fleece contains no lanolin, rain goes right through to the skin, but though they look miserable and depressed in wet weather, nothing would persuade them to shelter voluntarily under a roof. Instead they lay like tiny camels, backs to the wind, long necks stretched out flat to the ground, presenting as low a profile as possible for the elements to batter.

Luckily the storms were only a temporary blip and temperatures soon recovered, but it showed how careful one had to be in timing the once-yearly shearing in order to avoid any possibility of frost.

Alpacas have a life-expectation of around twenty years, much the same as a horse or cow, but although neither Meshak nor little grey Abed-Nego lived to be more than ten, in his seventeenth year Shadrach looks like a bony old man but he eats well and still enjoys life. His once-lustrous fleece has coarsened with age and is fit only for stuffing cushions nowadays, but over the years he has produced enough high-quality fibre to clothe the whole family several times over, not to mention blankets, rugs, cot-covers or anything else I had a mind to knit or crochet. Never was there such user-friendly yarn as alpaca. Devoid as it is of greasy lanolin, and beautifully clean without the chore of washing, it glides along knitting needles and leaves your hands with no sticky residue. Putting on a 2-ply alpaca sweater is like walking into a super-heated room – all warmth without weight – while 3-ply garments are, frankly, too hot to be worn indoors except in the most bitter weather.

Yet despite his long experience of shearing, Shadrach still struggles and 'urgles' like a two-year-old while undergoing the annual ritual and when, out of the blue, he suddenly throws a temper tantrum directed at his current companion, the fluffy, apricot-coloured Chimborazo, his blood-curdling screams and curses are still enough to put the frighteners on anyone within earshot.

CHAPTER SEVEN

The Frontier Tribes

Forgive the ant that steals a speck of grain
Like you, he lives with pleasure,
Like you, he dies with pain

Hindu proverb

FURRED OR FEATHERED, with two legs or four, with gossamer wings, or far too many feet, or just a single foot attached to a stomach, 'the frontier tribes' are what I call all the unofficial, unauthorised, uninvited residents of our smallholding. One can't say that they don't belong here since they were certainly in residence before we arrived. Like indigenous people whom ruthless invaders have dispossessed and pushed to the land's unproductive margins, they probably look on us as the interlopers rather than the other way round, and feel justified in mounting continual raids on our crops and livestock.

In response we wage long-running campaigns against them which we cannot realistically hope to win, for though we have access to powerful weapons, they are many, while we are few. They are single-minded while we can devote only a small proportion of our time to repelling their attacks and, most tellingly of all, they are active in the hours of darkness while we are asleep.

No one can deny that slugs, snails, and cabbage-white caterpillars, rabbits, mice, rats, magpies, grey squirrels, moles, crows, pheasants, foxes, badgers, deer, and all other raiders of crops and human provender have a perfect right to life, food and shelter, and I would be the last to grudge them a place on the strength if *only* they would limit the size of their families.

Some hope. Sharing, abstinence and compromise never enter the calculations of frontier tribes. With them it's kill or be killed, eat or be eaten, and in each of them the urge to procreate and fill the world with its own particular species is every bit as strong as the desire for food and shelter. If we did not keep up the struggle to whittle them down to acceptable numbers they would soon overrun the place entirely.

Any kind of farming disturbs the balance of Nature to some degree, and we are able to call the shots only because humans are at the top of the food chain. Everything we do upsets its regular working. Every time we intervene to protect a vulnerable species or one that is useful to us, whether animal or vegetable, we disrupt the plans of another in the intricately layered pattern. Ecologically speaking, we really should not consider whether any particular creature inconveniences *us*, but what effect our persecution of it will have on the other links in the chain.

Without wanting to sound too high-flown, I feel that all creation has an equal right to life, and animals cannot be blamed for following the nature they have been allotted – at least I do until the juicy, self-satisfied clucking of a magpie raiding small birds' nests in the garden sends such liberal principles flying out of the window.

There is something particularly sickening about seeing these strikingly handsome, bold, accomplished killers systematically working a hedgerow, terrorising chaffinches, bluetits, sparrows and blackbirds, who squawk and flutter in vain as their nestlings are dragged out and dismembered. Like

Vikings stripping a settlement, back come the raiders again and again until the nest is empty, when they move on to the next. Unless one intervenes to disturb them, a whole generation of small birds can be lost.

Magpies are clever, persistent, and extremely wary. They are under no illusions about the danger humans represent for them, and they have tried and tested ways to deal with it. When, incandescent with rage, I dash outdoors to stop the massacre of nestlings, they flip their wings and soar away to perch on a branch a hundred yards, sneering, 'Can't catch me.'

I know, and they know, that they have time on their side. I have other things to do, and can't stand guard over songbirds' nests for long. High on the branch, the magpie presents a tempting shot, but at the merest glint on a barrel or even the stealthiest opening of an upstairs window they will double the distance between us, while still keeping watch on the vulnerable nests. The glitter of a few old CDs dangling on strings might deter them temporarily, but the ever-moving, shimmering discs might also frighten away the parent birds bringing food for the chicks.

So what can we do? In my childhood, poison was the answer, though it now makes me shudder to think how many other creatures may have suffered horrible deaths after crunching up blown eggshells filled with yellow phosphorus paste, which we left out to tempt crows and magpies. Rodine, as that poison was called, is now illegal – and a good thing too – and instead we turn to the Larsen trap in an effort to keep magpies to a minimum.

This ingenious device consists of a wire-mesh cage about four foot square, divided into two unequal compartments. The larger has a top-entry door covered with a piece of roofing felt to keep off rain, a solid perch, and containers for water and food. This is where the decoy bird is caged. The smaller compartment also has a top entry flap, but this is springloaded and wedged open with a collapsible perch.

The male magpie has a strong territorial instinct and dislikes intruders on his patch, particularly in the run-up to the breeding season, so in order to lure him into the trap, you first need a live decoy, or call bird. Intensely suspicious of shiny metal or, indeed, any new equipment, he may have to be tempted for a week or more with small baits strewn casually around the general area of the Larsen before you begin placing them first on, then inside the compartment with the booby-trapped perch.

Down Mags flutters eventually, walking back and forth on top of the cage while eyeing the bait from either side. He tries to reach it through the mesh, then hops back to the ground to pace along the side of the cage, looking for a weak place. No go. It will have to be from above. Once again he perches on the lid, ducking into the open top, but the bait is still out of reach.

At that point – particularly if the would-be trapper is watching – instinct will very likely warn him that the whole thing is a put-up job. It may be a tiny movement inside the house that alerts him, or the semi-psychic way in which animals seem to sense the impact of a human eye. Whatever the cause, Mags decides that the tasty morsel is not worth the risk, and away he zooms to his favourite branch to think things over.

When this happens, there is a strong temptation to go and inspect the Larsen, perhaps to replace the bait with something even more enticing, but it must be resisted. The less Mags associates the trap with human activity, the better. In fact the best strategy is probably to stop watching the trap, get into the car, and go shopping for a few hours: more than likely in your absence Mags will make another attempt on the bait and, by landing on the collapsible perch, release the springloaded door and find himself trapped.

The next step is to transfer him into the more spacious next-door compartment without inadvertently letting him go. This is definitely a time to wear leather gloves. There will probably be a good deal of squawking and flapping, accompanied by some shrewd stabs with a very sharp beak, but once he is settled with water and corn he will accept the situation and hop around inspecting his new des res, while you reset the split perch and door and withdraw to a concealed vantage point a fair distance away.

Presently another magpie will come to see what has prompted his rival to spend so long at the Larsen, and most likely the caged bird will react by hopping on and off the perch and chattering angrily at the newcomer. This is just what the doctor ordered. I have seen four magpies caught in quick succession as, one after another, they challenged the decoy and ventured on to the booby-trap. Conventional wisdom decrees that you should then knock the first decoy on the head and replace him with the latest catch, because the last thing you want is a placid, semi-tame bird who does not try to drive off intruders. Some magpies, like some old lags, prefer a sheltered cage with food and drink provided to the uncertainties of life outside.

The best live decoy we ever had was presented to us by a judge, for whom this one bird had enticed seventeen of his mates to their doom. Judas, as we called him, was by then thoroughly accustomed to humans coming to replenish his supplies of food and water, and showed no tendency to pine. Indeed, he would greet his carer with the typical soft chuckling that so infuriates me when it signifies a raid on other birds' nests, and I suppose it is a magpie's way of showing pleasure. We grew quite fond of him, and he certainly earned his keep. So powerful was his attraction for other magpies that he soon notched up another nine victims in our paddock, and when at the end of the breeding season his strike-rate declined, we faced a dilemma. Glossy and plump after weeks of corn and cat-food, he looked a picture of corvid perfection. He had done everything we asked of him – and more. Surely, suggested my husband, he had earned a reprieve?

But if we set him free to repopulate the area with his progeny, all his work – and ours – would have been in vain. Reluctantly I pronounced sentence but, rather than disposing of the corpse in the muck-heap as usual, acting on a tip from a friend we wrapped him in newspaper, popped him in a plastic bag, and put him in the deep freeze.

Time and again that winter, as my hand quested for some fish or chops in the frosted depths, it emerged with a slim parcel which, on investigation, turned out to be Judas, and time and again I contemplated throwing the gruesome relic away.

Come the following spring, however, when courting couples of magpies once again began to terrorise the garden birds, we carefully defrosted the corpse, and propped him with twigs inside the Larsen trap. Battered and dishevelled he may have been after his nine months below zero, but amazingly Judas retained his old magic. Within two hours, his corpse had attracted a strapping new magpie and then, with the decoy succession re-established, we could at last allow Judas to rest in peace.

If magpies are the most rapacious of the avian frontier tribes, in terms of wanton destruction, woodpigeons run them close. The vegetable garden is a very important part of any smallholding, and although ours measures no more than an eighth of an acre, it provides far more food than all the ground dedicated to livestock, and inevitably attracts the envious attention of every non-human resident, official and unofficial.

The horses and sheep eye up the flourishing greenstuff surrounded by neatly-mown paths every time they pass that way, hoping that someone has left the gate open. Partial as they are to root vegetables, the sheep wouldn't mind a nibble of the parsnips, turnips and carrots, either, and the chickens long to scratch up the seedbeds. For this reason we keep it strongly fenced, with rabbit-wire dug in below ground level, and ordinary wire-netting to a height of seven foot. Nevertheless, with a wood above and a spinney below, it is still vulnerable to attack from the air.

It may be delightful to hear the gentle croo-crooing of woodpigeons: *'Where's your shoooes, Betty? Your blue shoooes, Betty?'* emanating from their hidden roosts among the leaves of nearby lime trees as one digs and sows and picks and weeds the vegetables, but the moment the coast is clear they seize their chance to launch daring raids on fruit-bushes, brassica, legumes and even well-netted strawberries before retreating, butter-wouldn't-melt, to their shady perches.

The woodpigeon, *Columba palumbus,* is a very different character from his relation the carrier pigeon, or rock dove, *Columba livia.* Not for Woody the heroics of Cher Ami, who carried a dispatch above the enemy lines in the First World War, and was awarded the Dickin Medal – the animals' VC – for delivering its tattered remains despite his wounds; or GI Joe, his doughty successor in World War II, who brought news that British troops were occupying an Italian town which the Allies were just about to bomb. Nor does he feel any urge to carry messages between New Zealand and the Great Barrier Reef, which the aptly-named Velocity, star of the Pigeon Post, traversed at the astonishing average speed of 125km per hour.

Far from it. While *Columba livia* is a sleek athlete who watches his waistline and performs amazing feats of endurance over great distances (and is fully protected by law), our friend Woody prefers to hang around at home, raising up to four broods in a single season, and eating like there's no tomorrow. It is hardly surprising that he tastes so good, since he feasts on a wide range of crops, picking out the most succulent and best of each. He is an early riser, and first light will reveal him snacking away on young cabbages or peas; just a nibble here, a peck there, and away he goes before the irate gardener is even dressed, let alone armed. Like deer, he spoils more than he eats, ignoring tough outer leaves, pecking right into the heart of brassica, or nipping off seedling legumes so that they wither and die.

When it comes to fruit, he is equally selective. Not for him the acid tang of gooseberries, but black, white and redcurrant bushes draw him like a magnet, and he will stuff his crop with raspberries until his neck looks deformed. In the same way cherries – just before they are fully ripe – are a particular favourite, and a peck into a plum will ensure that wasps can hollow out the rest, to make it unfit for humans. I have never seen a pigeon attacking our mulberries, which is strange, but perhaps he finds them too tart for his taste. Ripening figs, on the other hand, suffer the same fate as plums: a couple of stabbing pecks into their rich, juicy middles, and the remains left to the wasps.

Protecting our favourite fruits of the earth against woodpigeons demands much effort and ingenuity. There is no way we can net every tree or cover the whole vegetable garden, so it is more a question of devising spot protection for particularly vulnerable plants and crops. The trouble is, Woody is a shrewd bird. He grows wise to each deterrent in turn, and works out how to circumvent it.

Fine black cotton strung between hazel pea-sticks is effective for a time, because a pigeon dislikes colliding with the near-invisible barrier as he glides in to land. The drawback from the gardener's point of view is that long streamers of sagging cotton looped across the seed-bed make hoeing and weeding difficult, and close inspection impossible. Thus you may soon find that the crop so carefully protected from pigeons has been eaten by slugs instead.

Again, the flashing discs of old CDs have a mildly deterrent effect, though they add nothing to the beauty of the garden; and a gas-gun set to go off at irregular intervals will disperse avian raiders in a satisfactory hurry – until they realise that its bark is worse than its bite. An old-fashioned scarecrow, realistically dressed in gardening clothes and leaning on a fork, may keep birds at bay for a few days until some bold spirit decides that he makes a handy perch.

It is the old story: for crop protection, as for so many other rural chores, the farmers and smallholders of yesteryear had the best answer – while Third Worlders struggling to make a living from the land still do. Instead of sending small children to school at break of day, they are supplied with a bite for lunch, a stick and possibly a dog, and expected to spend the hours between dawn and sunset guarding the family's livestock and crops from anyone or anything minded to destroy them. How much healthier, more useful and character-building than sitting all day in a classroom! In our country, alas, there's no way now of turning the clock back, but as I survey the ruins of a row of peas, onions plucked from the soil, or a plum-tree despoiled of its fruit, I can't help regretting the March of Progress.

In my eyes, foxes resemble the Afghan tribes who caused such uneasiness to our ancestors on the Raj's North-West Frontier: feared, admired, but never, *never* to be trusted. They are highly skilled killers, bold, resourceful, and patient in pursuit of their prey, and they have powers of endurance even beyond those of a pack of hounds. I have seen a hard-pressed fox, confronted by a river, whip round and snake through his pursuers and the horsemen behind, to get clean away before the hounds could lift their heads and turn. I would *almost* swear that Charlie (as he is familiarly known) actually ran over the hounds' backs, but so swift was the manoeuvre that I may have imagined this.

Despite non-retractable claws, he can jump and climb nearly as well as a cat, tiptoe along rafters or roof-ridges to take roosting birds, and squeeze through the smallest aperture of a hen-house. Any weak spot in a poultry-keeper's defences will be found and ruthlessly exploited, with his trademark calling-card of a neat dropping with a cheeky twist at the point, deposited nearby to make sure you know he has passed that way.

Or you may be lucky enough to see him hunting field-mice, poised in balletic alertness, sharp nose pointed groundward, ears keenly pricked, ready to pounce when he detects the least movement in the grass. A vertical spring, a sharp prod of that needle nose into the ground, and then a rapid snap-snap of his lean jaws before he bolts it down.

Sometimes you may glance towards a sunny, favoured spot on the hill and see that the russet patch you first took for bracken is a fox curled at his ease, nose buried in his luxuriant brush, but though he is apparently dead to the world, in reality he is always on the *qui vive*, for he knows every man's hand is against him and can never truly relax in the open.

Besides, he is constantly on the lookout for his next meal. Being a scavenger, he can digest almost anything, and his diet includes as many beetles as mice, as many moribund myxy rabbits, blackberries, rotten apples, and decomposing burgers and takeaways as pheasants.

Even gamekeepers, his sworn enemies, can be made to admit that a fox is on a different level from the rest of the vermin they persecute, while men and women who ride to hounds treasure him as the mainspring of their sport, and never tire of embellishing stories both of his exploits and theirs in pursuit of him. They protect and preserve him, too, making sure that his earths are not disturbed during the breeding season. The 'Kennel Fox' who hangs around the flesh-house is a valued asset of many a Hunt, and can be relied on to get a home Meet off to a cracking start.

This rather ambivalent attitude towards an animal officially branded a pest finds an echo with most country-dwellers, for whom a chance encounter with a fox lends magic to the dullest day. As far as damage is concerned, it is arguable that by keeping down rabbits, moles, rats and other vermin foxes do more good than harm.

The urban fox is another kettle of fish altogether. It did not take long for this adaptable scavenger to realise there was an easier living to be had among the overflowing rubbish bags and restaurant slop-pails than in hunting rabbits and raiding henhouses like his forebears. Streetwise, traffic-savvy foxes find rich pickings in fast-food outlets whose meals are so often thrown away unfinished.

At first, when town-dwellers began noticing foxes in unexpected places, they were welcomed as an interesting addition to urban life. This perception changed, however, as the newcomers grew ever bolder and began to add pet rabbits, guinea pigs and cats to their diet. Outrage followed when a fox actually mauled a toddler in an upstairs bedroom, leaving her badly scarred; the assailant trotting quietly away before the horrified mother could do more than scream. There were the inevitable calls for town foxes to be culled, removed, shot, poisoned, exterminated... But how, in a great, crowded city such as London or Bristol, do you take such radical action against an animal who comes and goes like a shadow, and is thoroughly versed in avoiding human persecution?

Another unattractive aspect of the urban fox is his propensity to spread disease. Sarcoptic mange is a highly contagious infection, caused by tiny mites that burrow into the skin, making hair fall out in patches and setting up such a furious irritation that a mangy fox rubs and scratches himself raw. Unable to eat or rest, he loses all fear of humans and will stand staring aimlessly, the picture of dejection, until finally he collapses. From infection to death takes about four months, during which time he leaves tufts of infected fur in gaps and gateways where he has rubbed, and the mites are thus transmitted to any passing dog or cat.

The outraged urban dog-owner who discovers that Reynard has not only been frequenting his garden, possibly even bringing up a family behind the garage, but has also infected his pedigree pooch with fox-mange, soon stops putting out tasty morsels for this uninvited guest. Instead, he may well summon a marksman with a .22 rifle, who offers to rid him of foxes for a mere £200. Well-directed .22 bullets command a hefty price, but one which many a beleagured banker or mother of small children is ready to pay, and a bullet through the heart – provided it *is* well-directed – is a good way to dispose of mangy foxes.

Far worse a fate awaits the vixen and cubs who have established squatters' rights in the town garden of a little old lady. She dreads her Peke catching fox-mange, but she loves animals, she doesn't want the family shot – just transported into the depths of the country where they can 'live a natural life.' For an even more hefty fee, the fox-trapper agrees that this can be arranged, though he knows perfectly well that this means condemning them to a slow, cruel death. Foxes brought up on tikka marsala and chow mein will never have learned to hunt live prey. Nasty tales abound of farmers finding a dozen emaciated foxes in a single field, whimpering with hunger, and having to shoot the lot to put them out of their misery.

From Aesop to the *Canterbury Tales*, from the ballad of *Reynard the Fox* to the *Tale of Mr Tod*, the persona of the svelte, sharp-featured, super-cool trickster *Vulpes vulpes* has scarcely changed. No other wild animal retains such a grip on the human imagination, has inspired more literature, or been more widely credited with supernatural powers.

There is such an aura of mystery about a fox's secretive comings and goings, his quasi-magical appearances and disappearances, that it is no surprise to find him renowned as a shape-shifter in the folklore of many countries. A hunted hare in fear of its life is reputed to transform into an ancient hag, but a fox prefers a more glamorous metamorphosis.

According to the old stories, if you pursue a vixen over hill and dale, thorough bush, thorough briar, at last when the sun begins to set and your horse is near foundered, with her last strength you will see your quarry drag herself to the door of a neat cottage, deep in the woods, and slip inside. Aha! You have her at last. Flinging yourself off your horse, you hammer on the door and demand admittance, but when it opens you find no fox within, just a slim, smiling redhead at her spinning-wheel beside the hearth, and none but the sharpest eyes would detect the little white tag of a brush peeping from beneath her long skirt as she sends you on your way.

Outsmarting humans, outsmarting other animals, the fox is the ultimate survivor, his daring and cunning the stuff of legends. Even in stories like Beatrix Potter's *Tale of Jemima Puddleduck*, where his wicked scheme to eat both duck and eggs is eventually foiled, the thin-legged gentleman with black prick ears and sandy-coloured whiskers is still the plot's dominant character.

Given his reputation for wit and sagacity, it is sad to discover how vulnerable Brer Fox is to the guns and devilish wire snares of his only real enemy, and how small and slight he appears when trapped. Although he can change his plans rapidly when necessary, he has his own well-defined territory, in which his nightly patrols tend to follow the same paths, the same gaps in hedges and narrow runs through bramble bushes that he marked out when taking up residence. Inevitably the gaps he squeezes through bear the marks of his passage, and a running loop of thin wire secured to a tree or peg across one of his byways is all that is needed to catch him by the neck or pad as he slinks through.

To free a pad, he will gnaw through his own leg, and subsequently slowly starve to death since he is no longer able to catch enough to survive on. Should the noose be round his neck, however, he can do nothing but struggle until he chokes.

Walking along a grassy ride that led through a plantation of young hardwoods one spring morning, I heard a scuffling sound to the left of the path and, after listening for a moment or two, went to investigate. About forty yards into the undergrowth, I came on a flattened patch in the brambles, where a fox was lying, apparently dead. It was tethered to an iron tent-peg by a thin wire, stretched taut, which disappeared into its thick ruff. As I stood watching, the wire slackened slightly and the fox began to move. The moment he strained against it, the noose tightened again and, after a few convulsive heaves, the fox again lay inert.

I had nothing in my pockets with which to cut the wire, nor could I shift the peg, which had been driven deep into the ground. In its struggles, the fox had twisted the wire so tightly that I could not slip back the noose in order to remove it, and the only way I could see to free it was to pick it up bodily and rotate the whole fox enough to untwist the noose.

I was wearing leather gardening gloves, and the fox lay quite limp as I spun it round and round, but when at last there was enough play in the wire to open the noose it revived enough to snap briefly at my hand as I slipped its head free. Carrying it to the edge of the flattened brambles, I laid it on the ground and stood back, wondering if was too far gone to survive. The sun shone brightly on its muddy, dishevelled coat, long angular legs and the narrow jaw whose elongated, drawn-back lips wore a kind of sardonic grin. A lactating vixen, I thought, and felt a wave of fury against snare-setting gamekeepers.

For a moment or two nothing happened, and then in the blink of an eye she crawled with bent legs towards the sheltering brambles, slipped between two briar-stems and was gone, leaving me looking in surprise at the blood dripping from my glove. That one casual snap had cut right through the leather covering my middle finger, through the skin, and exposed the bone – but it was like being cut with a razorblade: at the time I felt nothing.

That fox probably survived. Not so the young badger I encountered on another narrow woodland trail. Again there was the telltale flattening of undergrowth denoting a prolonged struggle, but in this case the noose had caught Brock round the middle, and in trying to free himself he had bitten away most of his own back – a truly horrible sight.

It is absurd that it should be legal to snare foxes but not badgers, since both animals frequent the same territory, as do fallow, roe and muntjac deer – not to mention domestic cats and dogs – all of which suffer equally if trapped by a wire noose. Nor does the often-quoted legal requirement to inspect snares at least once a day guarantee the trapped animal a quick end: it may be twenty-three hours before the snare-setter makes his next round.

If in doubt, don't snare is the mantra repeated by the British Association for Shooting and Conservation (BASC) at every stage of its advice to anyone wanting to know where, how, and when it is legal to set wire nooses to catch vermin. But one man's vermin is another's treasured wildlife, and since the two are so easily confused, and snares are no respecters of species,

I should like to see the situation clarified by making *all* snaring illegal, with running nooses joining gin-traps, man-traps, and yellow phosphorus in the refuse-bin of gamekeeping history, where they belong.

The collective noun for moles is a 'labour,' and certainly of all our frontier tribes Moldywarp is the most industrious, toiling underground unceasingly and covering green pastures with a disfiguring brown rash. Not only the fields, either. Sporadic upheavals among the rows of vegetables in the kitchen garden are bad enough, but what really annoys gardeners and condemns Moldywarp to pest status is his determination to invade lawns.

Fertilised, aerated, precisely edged and mown to look like emerald velvet – the more perfect a lawn the better habitat it provides for moles. Worms are abundant beneath the shaven turf, and the soil is easy to work, so it is hardly surprising that given the choice between a stony field and a lovingly-tended lawn, the mole plumps for the latter.

Broadly speaking, female gardeners are less fanatical about lawns than men are, and consider the lovely crumbly loam of molehills, so useful for potting seedlings or as a top-dressing for flower borders, a fair return for the scarring of the green velvet carpet, but men value their lawns, and see the brown eruptions as a personal insult.

Many and various are the methods used to repel, poison, or trap invading moles. Some people swear by sticking toy-size windmills into the runs, which gives the perfect lawn a strangely festive appearance; others use solar-powered vibrators, which emit a low hum, but seem to make little difference to the moles; or drop strongly-scented mothballs down the tunnels – again with no discernible effect.

One really horrible method of control involves sticking razor-blades across the runs in the hope that the mole will lacerate his paws and, unable to dig, starve to death. Strychine is no longer a legal option, thank heaven, but controlled gas explosions are said to be effective, although you have to employ a licensed operator to set off the canisters of toxic gas, and I find it hard to believe that the process enhances the appearance of a lawn.

Then there are traps: old-fashioned pincers triggered by a pressure-pad, or the more effective modern equivalent of a short tunnel, from which snaps a metal band to throttle the mole, but both of these are often neutralised by the wave of loose soil which the mole pushes in front of him like a miniature bulldozer. This either jams the mechanism or sets off the trap prematurely, and in any case there is no guarantee that the marauding mole will use the particular tunnel in which the trap is set.

I find it astonishing that this muscular little barrel of an animal, no more than six inches long, can shift such quantities of soil so quickly with his spade-like paws. Though handicapped by poor sight, since he can barely do more than differentiate between light and dark with his fur-covered eyes, his hidden ears are acute, and the sensory hairs on head, forepaws and tail are extremely sensitive to vibrations above his tunnels. Anyone hoping to catch him at work must move stealthily.

Some – but by no means all – cats are good mole-hunters, but they do it purely for sport since moles, like shrews, have a disagreeably bitter taste. Such a cat will wait silently, ears acutely cocked, tail twitching, for the tunneller to approach, shoving his load of soil before him, and the moment the earth trembles and heaves up, a long arm with lethal claws is thrust down the tunnel to impale and scoop out the mole. This is quite a feat, since dense fur growing both forward and backward gives Moldy the ability to retreat as quickly as he advances.

With his cylindrical body, long snout, neck as short as any prop forward, powerful bowed forearms and spade-shaped clawed hands, his physique is perfectly adapted to his chosen way of life, but it is not a life I would wish on anyone. Digging in the dark, all alone, in four hour shifts round the clock in order to keep pace with his daily requirement of worms and other creepy-crawlies, the poor fellow has little time for social life, let alone T.S. Eliot's 'ecstasy of the animals'.

After finding a receptive female and mating in early spring, the boar mole reverts to single life for the rest of the year, in an existence which may accurately be described as 'solitary, poor, nasty, brutish, and short.'

The sow mole is hardly more gregarious. After her annual encounter with the boar, she produces a litter of four or five pups in a nest deep underground, and suckles them there for a month before evicting her offspring to fend for themselves. Thereafter throughout their three-year lifespan each mole crisscrosses his or her chosen territory, digging an ever more extensive network of deep and shallow tunnels, which they defend stoutly against interlopers.

I often wish I had some form of X-ray camera that could peer through the soil and show the pattern of diggings under our fields. Certain areas are most highly prized – probably where there is underground water – and it is only when earthworms are close to the surface that you can actually track one of these persistent sappers' route by the raised turf between mole-hills, and see that these excavations seldom run straight from mound to mound. There are branchlines and junctions, extra-large chambers for resting periods, and sloping paths to the lower level tunnels, which are maintained for use when the weather is dry and when worms retreat to the damper depths.

A dry summer is the mole's nemesis, and during droughts I have often seen their dehydrated bodies in the lane behind our house, where they have surfaced in the hope of finding worms and water. Each tunneller needs to eat roughly 70% of his bodyweight daily to compensate for his energy output, so if worms and other insects are unavailable even in his deepest workings, he quickly starves to death.

From our point of view these deep-level tunnels are beneficial insofar as they drain the soil and keep it aerated. It is the shallow earthworks punctuated by molehills that enrage groundsmen and farmers, for grass will quickly grow over the mounds, which then become impossible to flatten with a roller. The result is a bumpy surface that spoils any field for making hay or silage, ruins machinery, and trips up humans and animals – fatally, in the case of King William III, who was pitched over his horse's head when it stumbled over a molehill. It was an accident from which he never recovered, much to the delight of his Jacobite enemies, who used thereafter to drink the health of 'the little gentleman in black velvet' who brought about the king's downfall. Monarch, horse, and molehill are commemorated in a statue in St James's Square.

When the pups are booted out of the family home and sent to find their own territory, the sudden eruption of dozens of molehills which reflects this increase in population makes any sheep farmer's heart sink. To scatter the offending mounds with a harrow when the pasture is nearly bare makes it difficult for pregnant ewes to avoid ingesting loose soil as they graze, thereby risking listeriosis and possible abortions, but harrowed they must be if the field is not to be covered in lumps and bumps for the rest of the year. Choosing the right moment, when lambing is complete but the molehills are still malleable, is a matter of delicate timing.

Once the grass is growing strongly, however, moles and their workings become less visible and less of a problem in the larger sphere, though lawns are still vulnerable and a tunnel under a row of young carrots, for instance, is guaranteed to kill the lot.

By the time of year that vegetables are shooting up, however, another frontier tribe has usually displaced the little gentlemen in black velvet as the gardener's enemy No.1, and these are the voracious gastropod molluscs, aka slugs and snails.

Many and various were the goods, livestock, foods and artefacts introduced to Britain by the Romans, and great their civilising effect upon our savage forebears, but even Romans slipped up sometimes, and among their less happy importations, ground elder (to treat gout and rheumatism) and super-size snails (for eating) top the list. Like most non-native species – Japanese knotweed and grey squirrels spring to mind – both ground elder and snails have flourished in their new habitat and over the centuries have become ineradicable pests.

Take snails: no one can deny the beauty of their polished, many-hued shells, or marvel at the clever way they pack into neat clumps in the smallest crevices of drystone walls, or penetrate the dank interior of black polythene dustbins. How do they manage, encumbered as they are with that shell, to squeeze under the tight-fitting rim of the lid? Lift any stone in the cold winter months, and you will find hibernating snails, with all the soft bits drawn safely inside beyond the range of predators. Stand quietly near a herbaceous border in the warm dusk of a summer evening, and presently your ears will become aware of the steady chomping of hundreds of sharp, serrated teeth attached to the ribbon-like tongues of feeding gastropods, destroying the soft young leaves of hostas, delphiniums and lupins, nipping off stalks, and blighting the soil with their slimy trails.

It is enough to drive a gardener to drink, though it would be unfair and misleading to blame the Romans for all these gluttonous molluscs. True Roman snails are, in fact, quite rare nowadays, and enjoy a measure of protection. Dozens, possibly hundreds, of species of snail are native to Britain, and the huge population of slugs – black, brown, yellow, and white – is entirely home-grown.

So what can we do to thin out their numbers and protect our plants? Metaldehyde pellets are satisfactorily fatal, exploding the consumer in a little patch of silvery slime, but they are highly toxic and therefore cannot be scattered where there is any chance of dogs, cats, hedgehogs, or hens eating them – which puts the whole garden out of bounds. A more labour-intensive but subtle approach is to capitalise on the molluscs' sweet tooth, and trap them in jars of beer sunk to the rim in the flowerbeds. In they slither, and rapidly expire. What a way to go, the slugs' equivalent of drowning in a butt of malmsey!

Catching a dozen or so a night soothes the gardener's vengeful feelings, but it must be admitted that beer-traps make only the smallest dent in the population. It is much quicker to pick up a bucketful (wearing rubber gloves if squeamish) and fling the contents over the garden wall. The snag here is that both slugs and snails have a strong homing instinct, and marked specimens have been recorded back at base the next morning after slithering three hundred yards from the dumping ground.

What's more, the little blighters are hermaphrodites who do not even have to mate to reproduce their slimy selves. With slugs and snails capable of carrying about a hundred eggs each, and living between three to five years, the odds are weighted against gardeners, most of whom eventually admit the sad truth that no matter how many skirmishes they may win against this particular frontier tribe, victory will never be theirs. So grit your teeth, bite the bullet – and for good measure deposit a spadeful of gravel or chippings around your most vulnerable plants. Molluscs are not fakirs, and dislike slithering over a bed of nails on the way to their nightly banquet.

Grey squirrels and carrion crows are lone-wolf raiders, whose depredations are sporadic and seasonal, while rabbits and pheasants – so eminently edible – hardly rank among the frontier tribes.

Rats are a special case. They are the enemy within the gates, a Fifth Column that has grown so conversant with our ways and so closely woven into farm life that they interpret our intentions and read our body language as cleverly as dogs. They are, in scientific terms, metacognitive – able to solve problems by learning from their own experience – and a hoary old rat knows so many tricks and strategies that he can outwit us humans any day of the week.

Rats tend to draw into farm buildings in autumn. We don't often see them, getting just the occasional whisk of a long tail beneath a door, or hearing a scuffle on top of a beam, but I know they are ever-present, watching us from their well-established rat-runs in the rubble-filled walls of our old stone buildings, waiting to profit from a spilt handful of corn, or a few pony-cubes carelessly dropped over the stable door.

Frustrating their knavish tricks is almost a game. I know there is little chance of banishing them altogether, but at least I can make their life as difficult as possible by storing forage in rat-proof metal bins, and sweeping up left-overs. 'Where there are men, there are rats,' the Council Pest Officer once told me philosophically – she had been twenty years in the job and was thrice-divorced, so she had an intimate knowledge of both species.

Rats are expert at keeping out of our way, blending into their background, and covering their tracks. It takes a keen eye to detect the tail-trail flattening the dust across the floor of a shed, or smoothing a path through straw around a muckheap. Another classic giveaway is the faint sheen on the entrance to a hole that looks far too small for a rat to squeeze through, but has, nonetheless, been polished by the passage of countless sleek bodies. More concrete evidence of their presence comes with the discovery of their distinctive capsule-like droppings neatly cached in dark corners, or the holes chewed through nesting-boxes, usually at the back beneath the overhang of the roof. There is little a spy can teach a rat about living undercover, keeping a low profile and working below the radar.

Although it is difficult to like rats, I must admit a certain grudging respect for the way they make the most of their brains and unattractively humpbacked physique. They can collapse their shoulders in order to slither through narrow gaps, and their long, ever-growing incisors gnaw through chicken-wire and concrete with ease, not to mention the insulation of electrical cables. That long, corrugated tail is put to many uses, the most extraordinary of which must be in the feat – persistently reported though I have never witnessed it – of using it as a tow-rope. In a co-operative venture to steal turkey-eggs one rat will lie on its back, clasping the large shell, while the other tugs it away by the tail to a place where both can devour it.

I have, however, seen them stand on one another's backs to reach up to a swinging corn-hopper, or else descend the strand of binder-twine from which it is suspended. Experiments with lab animals have recorded the apparent altruism of caged rats who unfastened their own prisons, then released their mates, (though this is not unique to rats, since I have seen stabled horses do just the same once they have mastered the technique of lifting and sliding a bolt.)

They are good swimmers both underwater or on the surface, and despite living in some pretty unsavoury places such as sewers and muckheaps, they are personally clean, spending much of their leisure grooming their coats and combing their whiskers as assiduously as a Frenchman. So why do we shudder at the sight of a rat and shy away from contact with an animal that is so clever, unobtrusive, thrifty, industrious, and clean?

The answer lies in two D-words: Disease and Destruction. Though long ago cleared of responsibility for the Black Death by spreading bubonic plague, even a healthy *Rattus norvegicus* carries notable nasties which it hands on to humans with abandon. Rat bites quickly become infected, and Weil's Disease – the worst form of leptospirosis – can be fatal if not recognised in time, or mistaken for 'flu.

As for their destructive powers, few have described it better than Robert Browning:

> *Rats! They fought the dogs and killed the cats,*
> *And bit the babies in the cradles,*
> *And ate the cheeses out of the vats,*
> *And licked the soup from the cooks' own ladles,*
> *Split open the kegs of salted sprats,*
> *Made nests inside men's Sunday hats,*
> *And even spoiled the women's chats,*
> *By drowning their speaking*
> *With shrieking and squeaking*
> *In fifty different sharps and flats.*

Hamelin's plague of rats may have been in the fifteenth century, but over the following six hundred years their essential nature has hardly changed. Be it large or small, the rat population remains a feared and detested Fifth Column wherever humans live and work. In fact, if a modern Pied Piper ever offered to rid our farm of them completely – perhaps by mass drowning in the Severn – his thousand-guilder fee would seem cheap at the price.

During the hours of daylight, our frontier tribes keep their distance and limit their depredations to quiet moments when no one is around, but as night draws on, our authority diminishes, while those who can see in the dark become correspondingly bolder. Sometimes in the small hours a security beam will reveal a scurrying form crossing the gravel, or the nocturnal silence is broken by a sudden loud squealing, swiftly quelled, as some creature meets its doom. These are isolated incidents, though, and give little clue to the scale of nocturnal activity around the old buildings.

Snugly tucked up in bed, we can only imagine what is going on in the farmyard when the lights go out, but from snippets of evidence that I collect the following day, it may be something like this.

CHAPTER EIGHT

The Farmyard at Night

'SHE'S LEFT the hopper out!'

The excited squeak of a great-great-grandchild reaches Rattus Novegicus in his favourite lair in the crumpled paper sacks beneath the slats of a wooden pallet, but he doesn't move.

He, too, has seen Mrs Twolegs cross the gravel drive and go into the house without lifting the orange plastic hopper containing poultry corn from its hook and storing it in a metal bin, as she does every evening, but he hasn't survived as King Rat of the farmyard for over two years without learning a good deal about human body language. There had been something he didn't trust about the woman's movements, a faint but discernible ostentation in the way she glanced back before closing the door of the glass porch, as if inviting him and his family to take note of what she was doing – or had omitted to do.

The thick-walled stone buildings of the inner farmyard surround a hollow oblong of gravel drive, with the house, which is up a couple of steps on the southern side, commanding an excellent view of sheds, haystore, and stables. An open-fronted range has been turned into a white-barred dog-kennel, with the sheep-shed, henhouse, and muck-heap forming an outer yard beyond the stable archway. This is Rattus's fiefdom. He knows every inch of it: every hole and run provided by bales and rubble-filled walls and, by keeping his senses honed and his wits about him, here he has flourished on stolen provender ranging from black-bag overflow to the leavings of horses and sheep, and scraps from the human table intended for chickens.

There are holes he could have crept through in the farmhouse walls, too, and channels behind the wainscotting, but these he leaves for the use of mice. Though he is now too big for the house cats to tackle, there is always Jacko, the terrier, ready to raise the roof if he so much as shows a whisker indoors, and too many of his kin have died, dehydrated and delirious, after a visit from the pest officer for Rattus to risk stealing from Mrs Twolegs's own larder.

Half an hour passes, the light begins to fade, and all remains quiet. It is possible, he reflects, that in the matter of the hopper he is being over-cautious. From the bustle in house and yard that day he has deduced that something unusual is up. Cars have been moved from their habitual parking places and machinery tidied away. The haystore has been swept, and concrete hosed down, all of which indicates that visitors are expected. Perhaps Mrs Twolegs has too much on her mind to think of putting away the corn-hopper.

I'll wait until it's full dark, he thinks, folding his tattered ears flat and wrapping his tail around his feet. *She may remember it and come out again, or she may have left it in place for a purpose. I am old and wise enough to guess what that purpose may be, but it's no use trying to explain to the youngsters. They have to learn for themselves. Most of them will die before they grasp the lesson, but I can't help that. In any case, once Ratta's new family starts foraging round the corn-bins they're bound to attract attention and then we'll be in for another bout of persecution – traps, terriers, poison, our nests destroyed, no peace from morning till night – until things quieten down again.*

So he sits tight as the shadows lengthen, and the half-grown rats from the deep hole under the concrete floor edge to its entrance, darting out a couple of feet and back again, gradually lessening the distance to the hopper but always within easy range of their escape route. Even when the boldest of them reaches up to the tempting target, Rattus does not stir.

Despite the scars collected in a lifetime of dodging enemies, he is a large and handsome fellow, well-whiskered, bright-eyed and glossy. In his youth an inch of tail fell victim to a trap set exceedingly fine under a covering of straw, and constant battles for supremacy have shredded both ears, but for the past six months no other rat has cared to challenge him, either for a mate or the pick of farmyard provender, and his waistline has expanded accordingly.

His intent round eyes watch the hopper swing lazily as one young rat scrambles over another's back and clutches at its rim with small pink paws. Chittering excitedly, a third joins the pyramid and succeeds in hoisting its body into the shallow trough containing the corn. As if inspired by seeing this is achievable, its siblings follow, jumping on to the rim, grabbing a mouthful, toppling off as the hopper swings, and darting back to stash the booty in a dark corner behind the haybales.

Rattus twitches his whiskers. *Looks safe enough. Time I claim my share before those youngsters clean up the lot,* he thinks, stealthily inching forward.

As he does so, a white flash shot through with orange lights the yard, and is followed by a deafening explosion. Pellets rattle off the stone walls and the hopper swings wildly as the young rats scramble for safety. A few squeaks, then silence, broken only by scuffling and scraping on the dusty floor.

'Got one of the blighters.' Bill Twolegs's torch strobes into the hay-store. 'Oh, and look: here's another.' He picks up the pair of limp bodies by their tails and tosses them on to the muck-heap. 'Just about half-grown. I wonder where the big fellow is? I've seen Jacko telling to that heap of pallets, so he may be in there.'

'I'll let him out,' says Mrs Twolegs, and a moment

later the sharp-featured terrier races across the gravel. Fast as he comes, though, he is too slow to prevent Rattus's lightning slither to the rear of the pallets and into his hole, and by the time Twolegs has flung the top layer of pallets aside, Jacko has lost interest, knowing his prey is well out of reach.

'Leave it,' says Mrs Twolegs. 'I asked them for eight, so they'll be here any minute.' She unhooks the orange hopper and places it in a metal bin just as headlights scythe through the gate and a car drives across the gravel.

Reluctantly Twolegs re-stacks the pallets and whistles to Jacko. 'Another time, old boy,' he says, and strolls across to greet his guests.

Rattus lets several minutes pass before venturing out again, but this time he chooses a different path. The hopper had been a distraction only; he has plenty of other areas to investigate before dawn. Keeping close to the wall in case Jacko is still about in the yard, he slides round the corner of the stable archway and pauses before entering the right-hand loosebox.

The horses have been fed at dusk, and it is a safe bet that the pony in the left-hand stable will have eaten every scrap, but the old grey mare is less efficient. She is in the habit of plunging her nose into her feed and grabbing such big mouthfuls that a few cubes often escape and lodge under the manger where she cannot reach them. Rattus is wary of her big hoofs, which have more than once come close to breaking his back when she struck out impatiently at him. By now, though, she should have given up trying to nudge the stray cubes into the open, and moved over to her haynet. In a swift, scuttling scramble he is up and over the wooden door, landing on the deep bed of clean straw before the mare even glances round.

Now to check under the manger. He burrows into the banked-up sides and strikes one of his own rat-runs which the girl-groom has overlooked when she mucked out the stable. Here he is perfectly safe and his twitching nose tells him that the prize he seeks is there for the taking. Not only a handful of cubes, but flakes of maize and a few oats are scattered in the straw right underneath the manger, well beyond the mare's reach.

Better still, there is a stolen hen's nest in the corner, with three eggs in it. They are too big to be carried in his mouth, but Rattus long ago perfected the art of dribbling an egg with his nose, nudging it from each side in turn, and now he begins to roll the nearest one towards the drain through which he usually leaves the stable. Tonight it is half blocked by a wisp of straw, but there is still room for him to push the egg through.

A few inches short of the drain, he pauses, one paw raised, as his sixth sense flashes a warning. Why hasn't the groom swept the drain clear, as she usually does? Why does the grain lead in a tempting line towards it? Could there be a pressure plate concealed by that frail wisp, from which steel jaws will spring up and clamp his body?

Another inch, another nudge, and the egg rolls into the sloping drain under its own momentum. As it touches the straw, there is a terrifying clang that makes the mare leap back and stand trembling, legs braced backward, blasting air through her nose like a war-horse.

The egg disintegrates in a jet of sulphurous liquid. Rattus freezes, flattening himself to the floor, his heart racing. As the silence lengthens, the mare relaxes again, and heads for her water-bucket. Seeing him, she lowers her nose, snorts and stamps.

Get out, *you!* says her body language unequivocally.

No need to tell him twice. Rattus scrambles up the rough stone wall, runs along the top and down again to take refuge in the next-door shed where the chickens roost. Perhaps there'll be safer pickings here.

A stir goes through the twenty-odd feathered lumps ranged on the beams as he darts in short, rapid bursts along the wall towards the nesting-boxes, freezing to immobility when the fierce, red-wattled Cock of the Walk raises his ruff and gives an angry croak, running on again after checking the way ahead is clear.

Moving gently, Rattus eases into the broody's coop and listens intently. Her head is sunk deep into her grey-speckled feathers, her round eyes open but unfocused. She has been sitting for nearly three weeks, stirring from the nest only when the temperature rose enough to stop her clutch of eggs chilling while she hurried to feed and drink and defecate before settling back into position. Now she is listening to the tiny *chip-chip* of the chicks' egg-teeth working against the shells from which they will soon break out.

That will be the moment when, as the fluffy bodies begin to stir among her feathers, Rattus will insinuate himself beneath her, hoping to abstract a chick stealthily, silently, without the hen becoming aware of his presence. It is a risky manoeuvre. The smallest *cheep* of protest from his victim will bring retribution in the shape of a furiously stabbing beak. He and Ratta, working as a team, have managed it many times, but never without danger. Tonight, though, Ratta is busy with her new family and anyway, it is too early to attempt a raid on his own. While the chicks are still encased in their shells, he would not get away unscathed.

On, then, to the compost heap, which often provides enough decomposing vegetables to fill his gnawing belly, and after that it might be worth a visit to the dustbins. Loud voices and laughter accompanied by the chink of bottle on glass come from the house as he scuttles along the wall outside the kitchen but, despite the noise inside, Jacko registers his passing with a volley of barks which earn him a sharp reprimand.

'Quiet, Jacko! Get in your basket!'

From wall, to flowerbed, to tree, to wheelbarrow. A high, frosty moon has risen, and for a moment, Rattus crouches in the shadow of the slatted compost bin before clambering to the top.

There a pungent, feral whiff assails his sensitive nose. Someone is sorting through the contents before him, nosing through the debris, snapping out choice morsels – someone else the terrier would very much like to meet.

Wait and eat later, or risk a quick nibble? Rising on his hind legs, Rattus considers the scavenger, noting the sagging line of belly, the narrow neck and sharply angled shoulders. A gravid vixen, near whelping, probably too slow to catch him, though foxes are unpredictable: if hungry enough they would certainly crunch up a rat as big as himself. She has found the tufted crown of a pineapple and is delicately gnawing the fruity end while avoiding the spikes. The pared core may be close by, and that would be a prize worth eating.

He may be safe if he moves carefully without attracting the vixen's attention. Just to his right lies the hollowed-out skin of an avocado, for which he has a particular liking, plus one over-ripe specimen which has been thrown out untouched.

Too good to miss. Keeping the vixen's lowered brush towards him, Rattus creeps over the rotting cabbage leaves and potato peel and crouches down to nibble the greasy, succulent flesh inside the avocado rind, gradually relaxing as the vixen, too, continues to hunt for half-covered titbits. In preparing tonight's dinner, Mrs Twolegs has been extravagant, discarding nearly a bucketful of old vegetables, including half a basin of coleslaw coated in mayonnaise, grated carrot, blackened bananas, even a scattering of mildewed grapes...

Nosing back and forth, absorbed in his feast, Rattus is jerked from pleasure to sudden terror as a leggy, muscular dog-fox leaps lightly over the wooden slats surrounding the compost bin, landing almost on top of him.

For an instant he freezes, then scuttles frantically for cover, but Tod's reactions are too fast. Two slashing snaps, and Rattus's single long-drawn-out squeal is cut short by an expert, neck-breaking upward shake. Five seconds later the King Rat

lies dead among the kitchen scraps, a bumper portion for two hungry foxes.

This change in Tod and Vixy's luck comes just when they need it most. A den – hidden, dry, and well secured – has been prepared among the rocks of the old quarry above the farm's top gate, and two alternative hideouts have been scouted in case the coming family has to be moved in a hurry. Knowing the birth was imminent, Vixy had been reluctant to hunt that night, lying panting in her favourite sheltered spot among the brambles as the sun went down, and lagging behind her mate when he trotted purposefully towards the farm buildings as dusk began to shroud the valley.

Pearly dew is on the pasture, and young rabbits already venturing out of the hedges to graze, but the usual thick fringe of nettles stood blackened and bowed after a dose of selective herbicide, and Tod's attempts to ambush rabbits by getting between them and the hedge have been frustrated again and again. Aware that in this condition she is too heavy to catch even the youngest, Vixy has lain watching at a distance, her laden belly stretched to the ground, yawning from time to time, stretching her long narrow jaws to the limit, and uttering small moans of frustration and impatience as hunger twinges. Apart from earthworms and a nest of blind, naked mouslings, she has eaten nothing that day and needs fresh protein urgently.

Again she has lain watching from behind the low-hanging skirts of a yew-tree while Tod explored the haybarn, then bounded lightly on to the breeze-block partition separating the stables, and from there to the top of the wall beneath the roof. A maverick pullet had chosen to roost nightly on the girder supporting the A-frame, but she had prudently selected the very middle of the span, and after tiptoeing a couple of yards towards her, Tod decided that the girder was too narrow, the drop too great for it to be worth risking a twelve-foot fall onto concrete, and cautiously retreated.

By then it is nearly midnight, and as he crouches on the top of the wall, considering where to jump down, the porch door creaks open and light streams into the yard. A little unsteadily, Bill Twolegs comes out, followed by another man.

'Bed-time, Jacko. Here, Shep,' he calls. ' Come on, boys, into your kennel.'

Both foxes keep completely still. The old sheepdog would never bother to hunt them, but the busy terrier is an ever-present menace.

Paws patter and shoes scrunch across the gravel. Points of light from two cigars glow in the darkness.

'Beautiful night,' says the visitor. 'Just look at those stars. That's what we miss in London.'

'Here you are, good boys. Biscuits.' Twolegs shuts the kennel door and posts Bonios through the bars.

'When do you start lambing?' asks the stranger.

'Oh! Well, pretty soon. Officially they're not due for a week yet, but we've brought the ewes close to the house already, so Jenny can keep an eye on them. Keeps her binoculars on the windowsill, because she says they're just as likely to be early as late.'

'Well, I suppose that makes sense. People are, after all,' says his companion, laughing.

'Besides, the weather's always chancy in April,' grumbles Twolegs. 'Never know where you are – temperatures in double figures one day and hailstorms the next. We've built the pens, anyway, and I mean to bring most of them in on Monday.'

Presently the porch door slams behind them and, to annoy Jacko who is growling impotently from behind the bars, Tod sprays urine on the kennel wall then saunters across to the game-larder near the farm gate, where the drain often yields scraps of meat or congealed blood. Nothing doing tonight, however. The drain has been hosed down and the acrid smell of Jeyes Fluid overlays any aroma of animal blood or guts. Nevertheless, Tod deposits a neat cylindrical dropping with a jauntily twisted tail on the smoothly mown grass outside the larder as evidence of his passing, before moving on to investigate the compost heap...

When nothing remained of Rattus but his scaly, truncated tail, Vixy's energy revives, and she leads the way through the garden hedge into the steep, narrow lane behind the farmhouse. Cow parsley, with leaves just beginning to uncurl, fringes its banks, making a deep, defensive shelter for the hen pheasant who sits statue-still on her camouflaged eggs not more than a yard away from the foxes' keen noses, but Nature has so concentrated her body temperature beneath her abdomen that she gives off no scent to attract predators, and they trot past without winding her.

Nor does the badger who bundles down the steep bank into the lane, her mouth stuffed with white plastic netting from inside a silage bale, which she intends to use for bedding. Protected as she is by law, she has no cause to fear humans. Indeed, her decision to excavate a commodious sett under the floor of Mrs Twolegs's summerhouse might have been seen as deliberate provocation of the species which persecuted her family so cruelly in the past.

'Bloody badgers!' Twolegs mutters resignedly, as he trips over the ever-increasing heap of spoil. 'Why can't they build their houses in the woods and leave my garden alone?'

When the clumsy, lolloping figure of Mrs Brock disappears into the docks on the other side of the lane, the foxes shrink into the undergrowth as a car full of late revellers roars past them, its stereo system sending shockwaves through the still air. A hundred yards further on, they slip under the bottom bar of a stile into a narrow spinney, where their own threadlike trails weave between tall tree trunks and among young brambles which are just springing up, and will soon overwhelm the withering daffodils.

Their regular nightly round encompasses most of a neighbouring farm, where ham bones, deer carcases, or the remains of fallen stock can sometimes be found in a deep, illegal flesh-pit covered with branches, but tonight there is nothing worth eating, so they continue through the wood and across two fields, keeping in the shadow of the hedge.

From time to time Tod pauses to mark a tree or stone, warning off interlopers. This is home ground, well away from humans, and he threads his way confidently through the herd of bullocks lying on the edge of a low bank, and into the hollow channel between two boundary fences, only slowing to a belly-down crawl under the bare branches of an ancient oak, in front of which a semi-circle of brambles fringes close-nibbled turf to make a perfect nursery for rabbits.

Old and young, large and small, they bob in and out of the extensive bury on its edge, some with quick, lively movements, while others hop languidly, their eyes swollen with the onset of myxomatosis.

Softly as a shadow, Tod moves towards the nearest, freezing every time the rabbit looks up, stealing forward again when its head bends to the turf. One slow, stealthy step, legs bent, belly to ground, ears almost meeting... Another... Another, and he is within pouncing distance, his victim still nibbling unconcernedly, unaware of his presence.

Tensing his muscles, the fox springs, but his jaws close on empty air. In a single silent, deadly swoop the barn owl who has been sitting on the bare branch above drops on the baby rabbit, talons outstretched. Gripping securely, she glares round, mantling her kill with hunched wings, daring Tod to challenge for possession.

His brush droops as the adrenalin drains from him. He turns away, knowing he is beaten. There is no point in lunging at the owl: she will simply carry her prize back to the hunting roost and devour it there. Already her fierce beak has begun to tear the rabbit apart, and her leavings would hardly amount to a meal for one, let alone two. He looks around for his mate and gives a low call.

Vixy has taken no part in stalking the rabbit. Instead she has lagged behind in the sheltered paddock where Two-legs's thirty ewes are spending the last week of their pregnancy. Like huge powderpuffs with udders already tight and bellies spreading either side, they lie sheltered from the night wind by a stand of lime trees, propping their backs against the rough trunks, and take no notice of the vixen nosing round their trough in search of any stray high-protein cube they might have missed. Two-legs doesn't believe in wasting feed, however, and nothing at all remains of the carefully-measured ration he doled out at dusk.

The moon has set and a faint lightening in the east is announcing the approach of a misty, murky dawn when Vixy pauses in her scavenging and cocks her ears at a familiar sound. Jenny Twolegs was right: in the far corner of the paddock, under the hedge and as well away as she could get from the rest of the flock, one of the ewes has just produced a lamb, and it is the soft, eager slurping and grunting with which she is cleaning up her firstborn and urging him to rise that has attracted Vixy's attention.

Both foxes draw nearer and crouch, watching, but the ewe is far too absorbed to notice them. She is a first-time mother, guided by instinct rather than experience, and instinct is bombarding her with conflicting impulses: lie down, stand up, stand still, whirl round, look after this importunate white scrap that has appeared behind you, don't allow it to touch you...

He is a strapping lamb, quickly up on his wobbly legs, and he has a clear idea of what he is looking for, though less certainty about its location. For long, frustrating minutes he nuzzles blindly, too high, too low, at the wrong end, while his mother skips and pivots in small circles, sometimes urging him on, sometimes knocking him over.

The foxes lie immobile and intent, watching for their chance.

Five minutes pass before the ewe stands still and at last the lamb fastens on one of her small, rubbery teats, whisking his tail as the warmth flows into him. In response his mother nudges his back and haunches, helping him to bond, uttering little grunting rumbles, deep in her throat.

He loses the teat, finds it again, suckling more confidently, and finally sinks down between her forelegs while she licks and licks, drying the lanolin until his small fleece becomes white and fluffy. He tries to suckle again, but now the ewe is becoming restive once more, moving a few steps away, lying down with her lips pursed, nose raised to the sky and then standing up again, anxiously checking that her lamb is still close by.

Lying down, she heaves and groans. With every minute that passes, her whole being becomes concentrated more fiercely on expelling the second lamb, but however much she struggles and strains she makes no progress. At last one sharp little hoof emerges, then the nose and most of the head, but the second foreleg is tucked back, preventing the lamb's smooth passage to the outside world.

The foxes move nearer, but she ignores them. To and fro she threshes, groaning with effort, her struggles churning up the grass into mud, but to no avail. At last she stops fighting and lies panting. She tries to rise and collapses again, uttering an exhausted bleat.

The ram lamb bleats in answer. He gets up from where he was lying and begins to totter towards his mother, but with smooth, synchronised movements the foxes intercept him. Lowering his head, he stares at them, aware of their menace, then turns to flee.

Too late. A brief flurry of snapping jaws end his life almost as soon as it has begun. Each carrying a leg, the foxes drag the still-quivering body to the fence and force it through to the other side, their lips drawn back to tug and jerk as it snags on the squared wire, leaving giveaway tufts of curly fleece. Not until they are a couple of hundred yards away, out of sight of the farmhouse, do they pull the limp body under a hawthorn bush and begin to tear it apart.

Oblivious of her loss, the ewe strains again and again, but with each contraction her strength is ebbing, while the protruding head of the second lamb begins to swell and turn blue. Her struggles become intermittent, with longer and longer intervals between them. At last she gives up trying.

When the alarm goes off at six, Jenny Twolegs slides out of bed and flicks back the bedroom curtains. Sweeping her binoculars slowly over the recumbent flock in the Home Paddock, she breathes a sigh of relief. All lying together. All well – and today she will bring the ewes into the barn. Her husband may complain that it is too early, no lambs are due for a week yet and what is the sense in feeding them expensive hay when there is still plenty of grass in the paddock? But from her point of view it is too nerve-racking having them out in the open any longer. At least she is in control when the ewes are in pens. She is about to put down the binoculars and get dressed when she catches sight of a whitish hump under the hedge in the far corner of the paddock. Even at this distance the trampled mud all round shows clear signs of a struggle.

'Oh, God!' she murmurs, adjusting the focus and staring intently.

Pausing only to pull rubberised trousers and smock over her pyjamas, she grabs the bucket of lambing essentials from the chest in the porch and runs out into the misty field...

With her hunger properly satisfied at last, Vixy feels an urgent need to return to her den, and starts alone up the line of hedge towards the wood. Tod sniffs around for a soft patch of earth, which he digs up and buries the lamb's telltale remains in the hole before urinating nearby. The cache will probably be found and eaten by badgers, who care nothing for laws of property, but instinct warns Tod not to leave anything above ground. Then he follows Vixy into the wood, angling across the slope through the leaves of wild garlic until he strikes the path, rutted with quad-bike tracks, that runs all the way round one of the large release pens, which have been built along the edge of the field at the top of the wood. Constructed of tall posts and wire too high for any predator to jump, each pen is guarded with one or two high seats built into the first major fork of suitable trees, which reinforce the impression of a concentration camp.

At this time of year the pens are empty, shooting having closed in February, but in a month from now each of the regularly spaced coops will house a sitting bird, and already the gamekeeper and his sidekick are busy strengthening their defences, laying water-pipes and scouting for holes in the wire.

Having once experienced a terrifying jolting shock, Tod knows better than to touch the low electrified wire carefully strung between the path and fence, but like many wild animals he uses human paths where they suit his purpose.

Now he trots quietly along it to join Vixy, who has paused to sniff at the rotting carcase of a rabbit at the side of the path, her russet coat glowing in the sun's early rays as they filter through a network of budding beech-leaves. After a moment's investigation she lies down and rolls in it, squirming luxuriously as she works the pungent stench well into her shoulders and ruff to mask her own scent. Tod sits down and yawns widely, awaiting his turn.

Metal gleams dully in the branches above. *Phut! h*isses the silenced .243. An instant later, *phut!* again.

Grouch, the underkeeper, is a dead shot. After a moment he climbs stiffly down from the high seat where he has been watching for roe.

'Two on 'em,' he mutters, turning the dead foxes over with his boot, looking for signs of mange. The vixen is near whelping, her coat in poor condition, but the dog fox is in good nick. His pelt will be worth a bit, though he thinks there is no need to mention it to his boss, old Skint.

Whistling through gappy teeth, Grouch fetches his game bag from the foot of the ladder and bundles both foxes into it, then trudges back across the field to his mud-spattered Land Rover.

Dishevelled and pale but quietly triumphant, Jenny Twolegs is back in the kitchen before her visitors emerge from their bedroom.

She found the distressed ewe in the nick of time: another ten minutes and she would have been dead. After Bill Twolegs has carefully scooped her up on his tractor's foreloader and deposited her in a newly strawed pen, Jenny had managed to push back the lamb's swollen head, straighten out the bent foreleg, and deliver another little ram. Anxious moments followed until he could be persuaded to take an interest in life, and while Bill worked to revive him, Jenny fished inside the ewe and drew out yet another good strong lamb.

A large syringe full of the vet's magic potion – glycol, cobalt, and calcium – had miraculously resurrected the young ewe. For a few minutes she stands groggily, looking shell-shocked. Then her lambs' nudging and bleating spur her into action, licking and nuzzling their tails, and encouraging them to feed.

'Good mum,' says Bill approvingly. 'Incredible. Half an hour ago I'd have said she was a goner.' He looks at his watch. 'Should be OK now. How about some breakfast?'

Jenny leans over the pen. 'Poor lady, she's zonked out. What they all need now is a bit of p and q.'

They agree to say nothing of the early-morning drama to their guests.

'How did you both sleep?' she asks, pouring coffee, as – fresh, smiling, bathed and brushed – they come into the kitchen.

The visitors are effusive. 'Oh, wonderfully well, thanks. It's so blissfully quiet here. No noise, no streetlights, no sirens – just peace, perfect peace. We never heard a sound all night long...'

CHAPTER NINE

Fast Forward

Peaceful it certainly seems to humans, snug behind drawn curtains, unaware of dramas played out in the hours of darkness, the continual, intense life-and-death struggles that go on while we are asleep. Animals and birds that hunt and feed in the secret world between dusk and dawn must eat to live, they must kill or be killed, they must find a place to live and breed without, as far as possible, attracting our attention. That they manage it at all in an age which has acquired the technology to penetrate the deepest mysteries of wildlife: to peer down burrows and into nests, to capture on film the dive of a gannet, or follow migrating cuckoos from British woods to the rainforest of sub-Saharan African, is nothing short of miraculous.

Now and again as I go about my daily rounds I notice small signs that the night has not been as peaceful as it seemed to Jenny's visitors. She herself is going to be puzzled when she notices a newborn lamb's leg sticking out of a molehill some distance from the Home Paddock, and Bill Twolegs may well wonder how his rat-trap, set so carefully in the drain under the mare's manger, comes to have been sprung by an addled egg.

In the same way I see nibbled corn-cobs lying in the grass over a mile from where they are grown, or find a mildewed ham bone buried a foot deep in the soil of the herbaceous border.

Who put it there – and where was it stolen from? Greyish-white drifts of pigeon feathers hint at a sparrowhawk, while patches of soft, flecked fur caught on barbed wire show where a rabbit has been dragged through the fence.

Each of these small mysteries adds to my respect for the way in which our frontier tribes manage to carry on their lives and loves just beneath the radar, taking from us what they need to survive despite our efforts to frustrate them. It is true that they have more time to devote to robbing us than we do to exterminating them. Untroubled by VAT returns and diktats from DEFRA, with no need to shop or cook or drive or clean, foxes, rats, badgers, moles and their like are able to spend all their waking time single-mindedly pursuing their aims. We, on the contrary, fidget from one task to another, perhaps devoting an hour to it before hurrying on to the next.

As a result, we may be astonished at – for instance – the number of molehills that have blossomed overnight on the lawn, and wonder how such a small animal can shift so much soil in so short a time. Or how roe deer can massacre a row of runner beans, nip the leading shoots off fruit bushes, and strip off an entire bed of budding roses, all in the hours between dusk and dawn, or a family of badgers dig up two hundred daffodil bulbs over a single weekend, or the speed with which a couple of fat, elderly wethers can gnaw the bark off a quince tree to a height of four feet.

On discovering such outrages, one's first reaction is usually black fury, combined with a fierce determination to avenge the desecrated lawn, flowerbed, or whatever has suffered the attack with an array of nets, traps, barriers or foul-smelling chemicals, but as one's initial rage subsides, one has to recognise that not only do such deterrents look ugly, they also tend to be horribly expensive. Lion-dung will certainly keep deer off your roses, but scattered around the flowerbeds it quite spoils the scent of the blooms. In the same way, growing your own vegetables is no economy if you spend a hundred pounds protecting them with fleece and netting.

Should one then be philosophical – shrug and laugh and do nothing to stop the frontier tribes' predations, or is there a middle way? This is the question every smallholder must answer for him or herself and, gender differences being what they are, he and she are unlikely to agree. But neither of them would deny that the tribes' attacks keep us on our toes, and add drama to life's rich tapestry for, the moment we relax our vigilance, the jungle – both vegetable and animal – begins to take over.

Say we go away for a fortnight in summer, leaving only a caretaker presence to check that all the animals are the right way up, on our return we are sure to find that tough, opportunistic nettles, docks and thistles have encroached on every field, hinges have sagged and rails snapped; the best pasture will have grown shaggy and coarse for want of topping, and a riot of bittercress is certain to be smothering the kitchen garden. There will be a new audacity among the frontier tribes, too, as they include the house and garden in their hunting-grounds instead of keeping at a respectful distance, and it will take us at least a week of concentrated work to regain an acceptable measure of control.

Knowing how quickly our efforts can be nullified does away with any illusions that we are, or will ever be, in full command of even our small patch. Far from it, and – when not breathing fire and brimstone after discovering some felony against what I consider *my* property – I can't help feeling glad that despite our constant attempts to regiment and regulate Nature, her indigenous cohorts still have ways of striking back.

Thus in a never-ending game of Tom Tiddler's Ground, we and the frontier tribes share the resources of this smallholding and, were we content with a pretty basic diet, would harvest from it quite enough to feed ourselves, despite the inevitable seasonal dearths and surpluses. The difficulty is finding an outlet for the surpluses without becoming entangled in a mass of red tape.

Compare and contrast the case of today's smallholder with that of his jolly, self-sufficient counterpart of yesteryear, as he sang:

> *Let the wealthy and great*
> *Roll in splendour and state,*
> *I envy them not, I declare it.*
> *I eat my own lamb,*
> *My own chickens and ham,*
> *I shear my own fleece, and I wear it.*

Lamb, certainly. Chickens, on occasion. Ham, no. Free-range pig-keeping wrecks a smallholding for other livestock, and indoor pigs remind me of condemned prisoners, pining to leave their cells. Besides, their smells and squeals would rupture relations with the neighbours. We do, however, wear the fleece of our alpacas, even if we don't shear them ourselves.

> *I have lawns, I have bowers,*
> *I have fruits, I have flowers,*
> *The lark is my morning alarmer...*

Ah, now we're singing from the same sheet: half an acre of orchard and vegetable patch provides as much of what we eat as the rest of the property altogether, while the lark – or more often the current cock of the walk – makes sure we don't oversleep. Living off foodstuff grown on one's own land is a unique pleasure, worth all the work that goes into it, embued as it is with that particular quality that the French refer to as *terroir,* the 'essence of the land,' whose taste originates in one special, clearly defined place, and therefore cannot be reproduced anywhere else.

Thanks to the deep-freeze, meat, legumes and soft fruit often last us the year round, but luxuriating in *terroir*-grown food is necessarily a selfish pleasure, for it is when we try to sell what we don't need that our experience diverges sharply from that of yesteryear's jolly farmer. No shrink-wrapped meat or date-stamped eggs for him: he was free to rent a pitch in the local marketplace and sell to the general public without spending time and money battling with bureaucracy, and being compelled to upgrade his preparation and storage facilities in order to acquire the obligatory licence.

In his day, what was clean enough for his family to eat was wholesome enough for the general public, and he knew very well that if he sold any dodgy produce his customers would vote with their feet. Today, the opposite is true. Unless you turn professional and can assure a steady quantity of produce all year round, few shops are prepared to buy a smallholder's surplus eggs, fruit, or vegetables, while the meat trade is so tightly regulated that only your own family can benefit from home-bred carcases, and even they have to be precisely accounted for.

So our small attempts to make money from delicacies *du terroir* have generally been strangled at birth, one more victory for 'Elfan Safety' and loss to gastronomic diversity. The recent proliferation of farmers' markets is a step in the right direction, but even they are stringently controlled, with packaging, pricing, labelling and hygiene requirements too restrictive for amateurs like us to circumnavigate.

As a result, neither of us has ever been tempted to give up the day job, and anyway, running a smallholding is more a way of life than of making a living, since there is small hope of earning more than just enough to cover the costs. Even that requires some care. Buying-in forage is the killer expense. Between Christmas and Easter my feed bills always soar, but as soon as the grass grows again they settle back to sustainable levels. Seen as a hobby that can be fitted round the edges of real work, a micro-farm is much more pleasure than toil, a welcome break from desk and screen, and a constant source of interest, entertainment, and drama.

Taking your first sniff of the morning air, you never know what the day will bring. So much depends on the weather, the joker in the pack which no one can accurately predict. Will it be wet, dry, warm, cold, clear, misty, windy, still, or any of a hundred variations in between? Are all the animals you can see in their proper places? What were the noises half-heard through your dreams? Break-ins? Break-outs? The heart-stopping clatter of horseshoes on tarmac late at night, the scream of a mating vixen, or the hoarse screeches of an abducted chicken. There may be unlooked-for births, sudden deaths, disease or injuries striking out of the blue. There may even be miraculous recoveries or improvements in cases which looked hopeless. Whatever happens between now and nightfall, it won't be dull, nor is it likely to follow yesterday's pattern.

Originally part of the in-bye land of the great Cotswold sheepwalks that stretched from Burford to Gloucester, this little farm has grown and shrunk over the years as the fortunes of local landowners have flourished or declined. As recently as forty years ago it boasted fifty acres and supported a dairy herd, but now, whittled down to a mere four fields, it is little more than what estate agents call 'amenity land,' a *cordon sanitaire* of protection against encroachment by developers, and can provide only enough year-round forage for a small flock of sheep and assorted four-legged friends.

Watching the sun set over the Welsh hills from our top-field bench above the valley, I sense the ghosts of others who once enjoyed this vantage-point. Shepherds with their panting collies; journeymen on their way from Berkeley to Tetbury, setting down their packs to take a breather before tackling the steep slope of the escarpment, or pallid, crouchbacked weavers, blinking their watering eyes after long hours at the loom, as they emerge from their hillside cottages into the evening light.

Their gaze would have been drawn across the valley, as mine is now, to admire the long shadows thrown by the low sun on a patchwork of hedges and small fields, trees that lean away from the prevailing sou'-westerlies, and the shining thread of a slow-moving stream looping and twisting between rushy margins spanned by little humped bridges.

On the far slope, already shadowed by the hill, straggles the long, single streeted village where a few windows have begun to show lights. There are well-spaced, handsome stone houses built by eighteenth-century mill-owners, before the invention of the Spinning Jenny crippled the local cloth industry, and these substantial dwellings are flanked by narrow rows of cottages, a green, a pub, a shop, a church. Small figures stroll along the stream-banks, their chatter and the occasional bark of a dog floats up to me and my ghostly companions watching from the heights.

On a clear Spring evening the farmers and shepherds among them would have been checking their livestock, watching – as I am watching – the animals prepare for the coming of night, the lambs leaping and racing in mad games of tag to get their blood circulating before frost can crystallise the grass, while the ewes chomp stolidly in line from one side of the field to the other and back again, cramming their bellies as long as the light lasts.

Little remains of the weavers' cottages behind me but heaps of stone at the edge of the wood, with unexpected clumps of snowdrops or thickets of gooseberry bushes growing nearby, but the soil just below them is black and rich where their privies once stood, a boon to flourishing swathes of nettles. Their roots are deep, their vigour inexhaustible. Cut, pull, poison or strim them, and yet enough will survive to kickstart new growth as soon as you turn your back. No doubt our predecessors in the valley did their best to destroy them, too, but with no more success than we have had.

It seems a timeless, unchanging scene, yet to the ghosts crowding behind me this valley would have been a busy, noisy workplace rather than an oasis of tranquillity. In their day these lightly-grazed fields would have been thick with sheep contesting every fresh blade of grass, their plaintive bleating piercing through the background thumping of water-driven fulling-mills, their wooden hammers battering the woven cloth as the wheels turned slowly, night and day.

The river, now so clear, would have run scarlet with the dye for redcoats' uniforms, and instead of wafts of balsam poplar, the noxious stench of dirty fleeces immersed upstream from the mills would have poisoned the evening air.

There would have been many more people about, hurrying to and from the village on the well-worn footpaths, working men in drab, shapeless clothing, bonneted women and children in ill-fitting, hand-me-down boots. Plenty more farm animals, too: milking herds, beef cattle, useful all-purpose cobs and draught horses would have thronged the farm buildings, which are now used mostly for storing agricultural machinery.

Eight generations and two world wars separate that busy, bustling scene from the serene emptiness of the valley today. Though many of the same houses can be seen from my vantage point, some have shrunk while others doubled in size, becoming family homes geared for leisure and pleasure rather than places of work. Most of the field boundaries, however, remain just as they were two hundred years ago, as one can see from old maps of the parish, and some prominent aged oaks surely date back to the weaver-village's glory days.

So what will come next? Where do we go from here? New technology coupled with the ever-rising cost of travel may have brought us to an interesting tipping point. Will tomorrow's young men and women rebel against the boredom and expense of commuting to offices in distant towns, and decide to rebuild the weavers' tumbledown cottages and work from home, sitting at laptops instead of looms? Their brains and energy could revitalise the rural economy, and their needs bring new vigour to local trade as shops and services spring up to keep them supplied.

Or will things go in the other direction, with the last smallholders like us driven out of business by agricultural red tape and diminishing returns, our few pastures snapped up by neighbouring farmers and merged into large, machine-friendly fields, ancient hedges ripped out, windbreaks flattened, narrow, rutted cart-tracks turned into concrete highways?

Or will this smallholding descend into mere horsey-culture, the stone barns bursting with ponies and each field sub-divided into tiny paddocks separated by white electrified tape? Will the banky ground, suitable for nothing but sheep and wildflowers, be chosen as the site for concentration camps of intensively reared game-birds, untold thousands of beautiful, harmless pheasants and partridges which, after a few months of life, rich businessmen pay to blast out of the sky ?

There's no telling which way it will go, but were I to peer down from my cloud a hundred years hence, it's a safe bet that the view from our bench under the wood would be very different. *Autres temps, autres moeurs:* our successors will have different priorities, different mindsets, different ways to earn a living. Yet there would also be constants: the undulations of the stream, the gentle curve of the hills, and the square-cut solidity of the Iron Age fort above the village. No one is going to move that in a hurry.

There would be animals, too, and people working to feed and protect them just as we do in the age-old bargain between the species: *I'll feed you if you'll feed me.* Which of them was the servant and which the master would be just as unclear as it is now.

I would also be prepared to bet on the survival of the luxuriant swathe of nettles now flourishing below the old weavers' cottages under the wood. Everyone who has lived here has tried to eradicate them, but none has succeeded. Man proposes, God disposes, but Nature always wins in the end.

THE END

Further Phyllida Barstow titles from Merlin Unwin Books:

My Animals & Other Family £16.99

It Happened in Gloucestershire £7.99

Also published by Merlin Unwin Books:

A Beekeeper's Progress	£14.99
A Farmer's Lot	£12.00
Hoofbeats through my heart	£7.99
Living off the Land	£12.99
Maynard: Adventures of a Bacon Curer	£9.99
Moonlighting: Tales and Misadventures of a Working Life with Eels	£15.99
The Naturalist's Bedside Book	£17.99
The Poacher's Cookbook	£11.99
Shepherds & their Dogs	£14.99
The Way of a Countryman	£16.99

Available from all good bookshops
Full details on: www.merlinunwin.co.uk